Elder Abuse: Critical Issues in Policy and Practice

Elder Abuse: Critical Issues in Policy and Practice

Edited by

**Phil Slater
and Mervyn Eastman**

BOOKS

The editors dedicate this book with love to their respective children:
Lara Eastman
Nina Eastman
Mark Thompson-Slater

© 1999 Age Concern England

Published by Age Concern England
1268 London Road
London SW16 4ER

First published 1999

Designed and typeset by GreenGate Publishing Services, Tonbridge, Kent
Printed and bound in Great Britain by Bell & Bain Ltd, Glasgow

A catalogue record for this book is available from the British Library.
ISBN 0–86242–248–5

Bulk orders
Age Concern England is pleased to offer customised editions of all its titles to UK companies, institutions or other organisations wishing to make a bulk purchase. For further information, please contact the Publishing Department at the address above. Tel: 0181-765 7200. Fax: 0181-765 7211. E-mail: addisom@ace.org.uk.

Contents

About the authors

Peter Beresford is Co-Director, Open Services Project, and Reader in Social Policy, Brunel University.

Les Bright is Deputy General Manager, Counsel and Care.

Suzy Croft is Social Worker, St John's Hospice, and Co-Director, Open Services Project.

Mervyn Eastman is Director of Social Services, London Borough of Enfield.

Jill Manthorpe is Lecturer in Community Care, University of Hull.

Samia Naouar Ben Romdhane is Care Manager, London Borough of Barking and Dagenham.

Bridget Penhale is Lecturer in Social Work, University of Hull.

Britt-Inger Saveman is Senior Lecturer in Caring Sciences and Social Work, Kalmar University, and Senior Lecturer in Advanced Nursing, Umeå University, Sweden.

Christabel Shawcross is Head of Social Services Operations, London Borough of Barnet.

Phil Slater is Principal Lecturer in Social Work, Middlesex University, and Head of Student Unit, London Borough of Enfield.

Acknowledgements

The editors express their gratitude to the following people, in approximately chronological order.

First, to past and present staff of Enfield Social Services Group and Middlesex University School of Social Science, for the pioneering partnership arrangements that first brought the two editors into working contact with each other.

Second, to Jeremy Ambache and Martin Shreeve of the Association of Directors of Social Services, for inviting the editors to jointly address the ADSS's spring 1996 Conference, thereby setting the scene for the present collaboration.

Third, to Richard Holloway of Age Concern England, for first flagging up the idea of a book, and subsequently supporting the editors through the lengthy (and occasionally fraught) process of turning that idea into reality.

Fourth, to Ginny Jenkins of Action on Elder Abuse, for proposing the names of several less established authors, to complement and even supplant the more 'obvious' contributors.

Fifth, to all the English, Swedish and Spanish colleagues who collaborated on our parallel European Union-commissioned research into elder abuse in residential care, for reinforcing the belief that any credible addition to elder abuse literature must address the residential sphere via both a discrete chapter and integrated references throughout the book as a whole.

Sixth, to Alison Davies, Loui Fernandez and Nigel Hall of Enfield Social Services Group, for word processing advice and assistance.

Seventh, to Bill Taylor of Precision Engineering Plastics Ltd, for additional software and general computing expertise.

And, last, to Gillian Clarke, editorial consultant, for guidance and support in producing the text as now published.

Introduction

Phil Slater and Mervyn Eastman

Read not to contradict and confute,
nor to believe and take for granted
. . . but to weigh and consider.

(Francis Bacon, 1561–1626)

The 1990s have witnessed a significant growth of interest in the phenomenon previously referred to as 'old age abuse' and currently known as 'elder abuse'. A measure of this development is the exponential growth of written material on the subject, covering the full range of books, articles, research reports, official guidance and assorted pamphlets.

The scale of this literary enterprise is indicated by the contrasting lengths of the first and second editions of an overview published by the Age Concern Institute of Gerontology within a mere five years of each other: 60-odd pages in the first instance (McCreadie, 1991), and exactly double in the second (McCreadie, 1996). In the latter case, the references section alone runs to eleven pages of closely typed text. On a personal note, the author reveals that, when she undertook to produce the second edition, 'I scarcely realised the scale of the task that was awaiting me' (McCreadie, 1996, p v).

The expanding range and breadth of publications on elder abuse is generally considered to be 'a good thing'. At a time when educationalists and popular commentators point to a decline not only in reading habits but also even in the acquisition of reading skills themselves, a growing market in serious reading matter in any field is welcome. This is doubly true in the case of a body of literature whose growth is generally attributed to an increasing concern about the quality of life of our older citizens and appropriate policies to support them, in some instances to care for them and in extreme cases to protect them (McCreadie, 1996, p vi).

Nevertheless, or perhaps for this very reason, would-be contributors to the expanding body of elder abuse literature would be well advised to stand back and consciously reflect on the rationale of their particular project. What precisely is the author's message, and what, if anything, is new about it? In what ways does the presentation differ from that of existing works on the subject, and why has this particular approach been taken? Most important of all, how do the authors see their work contributing to society's appreciation of a complex phenomenon that goes to the heart of what it means to be a human being living in a civilised society?

Existing books on elder abuse can be understood as occupying particular locations on a non-hierarchical spectrum. At one end of the continuum, authors devote their attention to the single-minded exploration of one particular aspect of the phenomenon, for example *Gender Issues in Elder Abuse* (Aitken and Griffin, 1996). At the opposite end of the continuum, an attempt may be made to relocate elder abuse in general within a broader context, as most notably in the case of *Family Violence and the Caring Professions* (Kingston and Penhale, 1995). The mid-point between these two extremes is occupied by authors who accept elder abuse as a relatively discrete phenomenon and who aim to 'provide the reader with the accumulated knowledge base concerning this obviously complex human experience' (Bennett et al, 1997, p 1).

In contributing to the growing literature on elder abuse, the present collection of chapters is bound to revisit much of the territory and many of the arguments of books already published on the subject. Nevertheless, the editors have no desire to compete with the existing introductory texts (in addition to Bennett et al, 1997, see Eastman, 1994, and Decalmer and Glendenning, 1997). Neither is the present collection constructed in the manner of an elder abuse 'manual', least of all one that aspires to definitive status in the field. Such an enterprise would not merely suggest personal conceit but would simultaneously bear witness to a lack of appreciation of the necessarily rudimentary state of professional practice in the absence of national policy guidelines and uniform legislative provision.

In direct contrast to a manual, the present text does not aim to distil the essential components of a supposedly coherent and unproblematical whole, but rather to amplify the dilemmas and contradictions inherent in the construction of 'elder abuse' as a social problem. As the subtitle makes clear, the strategic focus is on critical issues in policy and practice, with particular regard to their complex interrelationship. The nature and range of the issues addressed in the various chapters are readily indicated by the Contents page. By way of introduction, however, it is important to clarify what is (and is not) meant by 'critical' in the present context.

The first and most common association with the word 'critical', as confirmed by the *Oxford English Dictionary*, is of fault-finding or 'censoriousness'. By way of illustration, the 'critical' debate among rival political parties frequently boils down to the simple repudiation of a given view as 'wrong', coupled with an assumption of the contrary view as 'right'. With reference to elder abuse, one memorable example of such a 'critical' contribution appeared in the British trade journal, *Community Care* (North, 1997), where a highly respected national campaigning body (Action on Elder Abuse) was berated for inappropriate client group definition (excluding non-elderly adults) and narrowly constrained models of explanation and intervention (allegedly 'medical' and 'anti-social work').

The issues of client nomenclature and professional models are most certainly important; indeed, they are explored at some length in the present book. However, reduced to the level of bald assertions, unsubstantiated by reasoned argument adequate to the complexities of the matter, the *Community Care* episode offers a convenient example of the sort of 'critical' intervention that is most certainly not the approach taken by the contributors to the present collection of chapters.

At the opposite extreme from the 'demolition job', Western philosophers (from Kant to Sartre) have associated the 'critical' spirit with systematic examination of a given phenomenon so as to clearly establish its essential nature, extent and ultimate limits. With specific reference to elder abuse, such a spirit is evident in the declaration of two distinguished North American writers:

> Elder abuse does appear to us to constitute a distinct category of abuse, worthy of special attention. Such classification is justified by the special characteristics of the elderly, which affect their vulnerability to abuse and the nature of the abuse they suffer, and also by the nature of society's relationship to older persons ... It is our belief that older persons are especially vulnerable to certain kinds of maltreatment at the hands of family members, that this maltreatment can be defined and measured, and that the success of various interventions can be evaluated. (Wolf and Pillemer, 1989, pp 13ff)

Importantly, this 'critical' intent is not merely enunciated but is also substantiated in the text it introduces.

However, such an approach is not without its limitations. In particular, its exponents conceive of their intellectual efforts in purely 'scientific' terms, failing to register the significance of the social structures that sustain such intellectual processes, let alone to explore the reciprocal effects of those processes on existing social structures generally. By contrast, 'radical' concerns of this nature are at the very heart of the third and final variant of 'critical' thinking, as pioneered by Marx and Engels in the 1840s and subsequently absorbed (albeit in watered down form) into mainstream intellectual thought under the auspices of the 'sociology of knowledge'.

With reference to elder abuse, critical thinking along specifically sociological lines has favoured Blumer's model of 'social problem construction', according to which:

> Social problems are not the result of an intrinsic malfunctioning of a society, but are the result of a process of definition in which a given condition is picked out and defined as a social problem ... A social problem exists primarily in terms of how it is defined and conceived in a society, instead of being an objective condition with a definitive objective makeup. The societal definition, and not the objective makeup of a given social condition, determines whether the condition exists as a social problem. The

societal definition gives the social problem its nature, lays out how it is to be approached, and shapes what is done about it. (Blumer, 1971, pp 300ff)

The process itself is characterised by distinct stages, each involving specific social activities: emergent discussion of a novel problem, official legitimisation as a problem, mobilisation of action, formation of an official plan, and implementation of the plan through designated channels, involving evaluation of outcomes and reconsideration of the terms of reference of the original problem.

Blumer's model has been particularly popular with the more sociologically minded contributors to elder abuse literature. In North America, for example, Leroux and Petrunik (1990) published a one-off application of the model to developments in Canada. Across the Atlantic, the same model has been deployed to gauge progress in Britain from the early stages of emergence/legitimisation (Bennett and Kingston, 1993) to the significantly advanced stage of official plan formation, prompting the question 'whether the final stage, that of implementation of the plan for action, will be achieved' (Bennett et al, 1997, p 14).

All in all, Blumer's model has contributed to the illumination of elder abuse as a problem in the process of social construction, directing particularly critical attention to the activity (and relative inactivity) of national and local policy makers. At the same time, it must be acknowledged that the model is relatively modest in its scope and thus inevitably inadequate to the myriad social complexities of elder abuse at the interface between individuals, social groups and the state. Crucially, the model is oblivious not only to the unequal distribution of social power (including the power to define a problem in the first place) but also, not surprisingly, to the reciprocal effects of 'official' action plans in reproducing such power differentials.

By way of dramatic contrast, a radically expanded social perspective is illustrated by a theoretical contribution indicatively titled 'Social policy as elder abuse', which explicitly propounds a 'strong' argument:

The 'discovery' of abuse specifically aimed at older people must be placed against a policy background in which vulnerable elders are perceived as a burden and the costs of care, both fiscal and emotional, are being transferred from the state to families and friends ... An emphasis on monitoring, in the absence of any serious policy initiative to discover a carer's suitability or willingness to care, constitutes a form of surveillance, and the call for more powers of intervention a bigger stick with which to beat carers who will not conform. The 'discovery' of abuse therefore empowers the policing of informal care. (Biggs, 1997, p 75)

Of particular significance at the present juncture is the author's claim that current elder abuse debates are in desperate need of such 'critical analysis' (as Biggs himself terms it) if the competing interests of users, carers, professionals, society in general and the state at large are to be adequately addressed, let alone satisfactorily accommodated.

The present book comprises nine original contributions to this 'critical' project. In Chapter 1, Bridget Penhale critically reviews existing research on elder abuse, aiming to distil lessons for practice analogous to the UK's *Child Protection: Messages from research* (Department of Health, 1995), although the relative underdevelopment of elder abuse as a social problem (a state of affairs itself subject to critical evaluation) means that her findings are inevitably of more modest proportions in this regard. Jill Manthorpe, in Chapter 2, then retraces the history and achievements of social campaigning, from the early days of 'old age abuse' to the present work of Action on Elder Abuse, concluding with an argument for enhanced 'personal/political' (particularly feminist) considerations of elder abuse. The view of elder abuse as an objective 'thing' thus gives way to a complex analysis of conflicting social forces; this shift takes the reader to the heart of the book's overall critical intention.

In Chapter 3, Phil Slater explores in greater detail the specific question of the appropriateness (or otherwise) of organising social campaigns around a particular age group, and considers the critical relevance of parallel initiatives related to vulnerable adults generally. Christabel Shawcross, in Chapter 4, turns the spotlight on the strategic need for, and varied experience of attempts to develop, local policies on a joint inter-agency basis, led but not dominated by local authorities. This leads directly into Chapter 5, where Suzy Croft and Peter Beresford reiterate the vital importance of ensuring that developments in the study and prevention of elder abuse are characterised by genuine user participation at the twin levels of general policy and direct practice. In doing so, they elaborate on a critical theme flagged up in earlier chapters and revisited throughout the remainder of the book.

Chapter 6 presses deeper into the policy sphere, with Mervyn Eastman uncovering a predominantly medical model in popular understandings of, and professional interventions in, elder abuse, arguing passionately for the reassertion of a social model at both levels. Phil Slater and Samia Naouar Ben Romdhane jointly contribute Chapter 7, which simultaneously explores the critical relevance of such a model to professional education and offers a highly challenging case study drawn from direct social work practice. Chapter 8, by Les Bright, explores the issue of detection and prevention in residential/nursing home settings, arguing that the continued marginalisation of this area has more to do with wilful disregard than with any supposed lack of available evidence. Once again, the critical thrust of the book as a whole is powerfully re-emphasised. Finally, in Chapter 9, Britt-Inger Saveman revisits many of the themes and arguments of the previous chapters from a specifically international perspective, concluding with a sober reminder of what elder abuse is actually about: human suffering and social responsibility!

The particular mix of contributing authors (many of whom will already be familiar to readers) is itself significant. In commissioning chapters sharing a common critical perspective, the editors had not merely to identify a coherent range of issues, but also to assemble a team of contributors in some degree representative of the stakeholders engaged in constructing elder abuse as a social problem.

Of the contributors to this book, including its editors, exactly half hold front-line or managerial posts in a range of statutory and independent agencies, and have substantial additional experience of campaigning in various areas of social welfare and/or civil rights. The other half, while formally appointed to academic posts, are qualified professionals who have maintained close links with, or even direct involvement in, practice agencies and/or campaigning organisations. Twin themes in all contributors' work have been the integration of theory and practice and the promotion of genuine 'user' power.

Extending the range of contributors beyond a narrowly defined academic circle raises a critical issue in its own right: editorial tolerance of heterogeneous writing styles. This was dramatically illustrated in the case of a collection of chapters published under the title *Empowerment in Community Care* (Jack, 1995), on which many of the present contributors collaborated. The editor confronted the issue of stylistic tolerance head-on:

> What would be the point of publishing a text on empowerment which disempowered its contributors by insisting on a uniformity of language and style and demanding adherence to conventions governing the communication of ideas? Although approved of by academic custom, these conventions are alien to several of the authors and much of the potential readership. (Jack, 1995, p 5)

Exactly the same is true of the present collection of chapters. As one colleague pointed out in the early stages of commissioning, an author who spends a significant part of his time in intensive work with care assistants (a strategic priority in elder abuse developments) will almost certainly express himself differently from a university lecturer working predominantly with social work students. Thus, a book that aims to reflect the social spectrum of elder abuse stakeholders in its collective authorship must be prepared to accommodate a representative range of writing styles.

In commissioning the various chapters, however, the editors sought to promote common standards of content, as opposed to style. First, all authors were asked to survey the existing literature pertinent to their particular area of expertise, albeit with scope for divergent levels of direct quotation. Secondly, while perfectly at liberty to make appropriate use of personal anecdote, contributors were expected to offer a coherent analysis of their respective subject matter. Thirdly, all chapters were to feature explicit consideration of the implications for emerging practice. Inevitably, execution of the original briefs generated occasional repetition of detail, together with both overlaps and divergences in specific arguments. No attempt has been made to edit these out.

As finally presented to a, we hope, concerned public, the book makes no claims to being either comprehensive in its overall coverage or definitive in its individual contributions. Indeed, any such pretensions would contradict the critical spirit at the heart of the project. Rather, the book is offered as a contribution to the understanding and management of a serious social problem. The authors' arguments cannot in good faith be dismissed lightly, but, if they prompt others to more coherent considerations with a view to more effective interventions, the critical intention of the book will have been fulfilled.

As Sir Isaiah Berlin, one of the greatest philosophers of the twentieth century, pointed out, genuine commitment to a social cause is characterised by the assumption of robust arguments in tandem with an acknowledgement of their necessarily limited validity and a confident acceptance of both the inevitability and the desirability of a critical response from others. The pursuit of absolute certainty, by contrast, may well satisfy a deep human need, 'but to allow it to determine one's practice is a symptom of an equally deep, and more dangerous, moral and political immaturity' (Berlin, 1969, p 172).

Researching elder abuse: lessons for practice

Bridget Penhale

The abuse of older people is a phenomenon that is increasingly recognised. It has been much researched and written about in North America, but considerably less so in the UK. The 1990s have seen an increase in interest in the UK, but not the moral panic and public outcry that accompanied the 'discovery' of child abuse in earlier decades. Among the reasons for this must surely be the ageist attitudes that permeate society. Gender issues also operate within this paradigm, particularly as the majority of people who are abused are women – to an extent that is greater than simply the fact that there are more older women than older men. Researchers who investigate family violence have also become interested in elder abuse, although there would seem to be important differences between the various forms of domestic violence and these may prove to be more pertinent than the commonalties (Penhale, 1993).

One of the areas that has proved to be somewhat problematic in the past has been in the definition of abuse. There has been no agreement between either researchers or, in North America, legislators as to what constitutes abuse and neglect; it is therefore difficult to extrapolate generalisations (about the incidence, prevalence and other characteristics of the phenomenon) from the research findings that will be of direct use in the future. Neither is it certain how well such findings travel cross-culturally. Moreover, much of the research that has been carried out tends to be of fairly small, unrepresentative, samples of victims, and many do not include any form of control group, so there are methodological difficulties both in the way that the research is conducted and also in the validity of the interpretation of the results.

This chapter considers the major findings that have become available in recent years about elder abuse from both a UK and an international perspective. Whilst the USA has in some respects dominated the field to date, important research is happening elsewhere – Australia, Canada, Scandinavia and the Netherlands, to name a few areas. It is important that these findings are available to practitioners in a way that is accessible to them. The chapter opens with a consideration of the difficulties in conducting research in this area, including an examination of some of the ethical dimensions that must be covered. It then reports on the major findings from the UK and elsewhere, considering the principal lessons to be drawn from the practitioner's perspective. Consideration is also given to issues concerning the dissemination of research findings and the need to establish appropriate networks for the exchange of information about both research and best practice in this field.

The last part of the chapter focuses on some of the reasons why in the UK we do not yet have a document equivalent to the Department of Health publication *Child Protection: Messages from research* (1995) and considers some of the prerequisites for the production of such a document. Finally, the development of a research agenda in national terms is considered and suggestions are made.

Researching elder abuse

Since the mid-1970s, there has been a focus in North America on research into elder abuse. Although the issue was identified in the UK at about the same time, it was not until the late 1980s that research into elder abuse and neglect really began to happen in this country.

There is still a great deal of controversy, however, about such issues as definitions of elder abuse, indicators of abuse and the role of neglect in considerations of abuse. In many respects, research in this area is still in its infancy in the UK and, because of the lack of any overall national research strategy, it is likely that further small-scale studies are taking place without any coherent overall view as to the continued usefulness of such an approach.

What this may lead to is a situation in which there is a question mark over the potential value of further research work, as the validity and reliability of each completed piece of research may be disputed. The principal reasons for this are that different research projects tend to look at slightly different aspects of the problem and use differing methodologies and small-scale samples. Comparing data from the different research findings may then become virtually impossible and can almost make the concept of elder abuse meaningless for researchers and for the general public.

Research into other forms of family violence has incurred similar problems (Chelucci and Coyle, 1992). However, the abuse of children and of younger women in domestic situations from men known to them have been established as social problems for some years (the past two decades in relation to matters of child protection, and the past decade with regard to domestic violence). Therefore, the very real difficulties in researching such sensitive areas do not seem to have influenced the development of social concern in the same way as might appear to be happening with elder abuse. However, even these fields are not without difficulty in research terms. For example, in a review, Weiss commented on the substantial discrepancies among estimates of the prevalence, incidence and correlates of family violence, which might suggest that the value of the research results is compromised (Weiss, 1988); for these reasons, questions were raised about the reliability of estimates of child abuse (Taylor, 1989).

In his research review concerning elder abuse, Ogg states:

> Elder abuse in Britain is emerging as a social problem not on the basis of empirical research but on account of action within the social and health

care professions based on the anecdotal evidence of many forms of elder abuse in several diverse settings. (Ogg, 1993, p 37)

Ogg and others are concerned that a large number of health and social agencies are actively devising strategies or guidelines regarding the identification, intervention and prevention of elder abuse in the absence of firm knowledge derived from research. Two broad areas in the research process can be analysed further to give some insight into the difficulties encountered:

- methodological difficulties in developing indicators of abuse;
- ethical issues about self-disclosure/victimisation.

It is necessary to consider each of these areas in turn.

Methodological difficulties

The first aim of the researcher is to develop the questions that need to be answered and to formulate a hypothesis. This is comparatively easy when dealing with concrete forms of abuse such as physical and some situations of sexual abuse, but much more difficult with less tangible areas such as psychological abuse or abusive situations that involve comparative behaviour patterns. In addition, it is important to be aware of the influence of attitudes, societal norms and structural concomitants such as ageism, which may have a bearing on situations that are, or may be construed as, abusive. Ogg has set out research principles for the study of elder abuse that can be summarised thus:

- Older people have the legal and moral right to self-determination.
- They have the right to protection from harm or exploitation.
- There is no consensus on the respective roles of the state and family in the care of dependent older people.
- Domestic violence often continues into old age. (Ogg, 1993)

Ogg's first three points highlight the differences that are present between differing groups. Children are generally perceived within society as a vulnerable group in need of extensive protection. In connection with this perception, the statutory and legal framework consolidated in the Children Act 1989 has protective functions towards children, who as minors have limited decision-making or choice-making capacity in legal terms.

Mentally competent older people often choose to remain in abusive circumstances. This may be in the face of strong pressure from health and social services workers to the contrary. The reasons for staying in such situations are undoubtedly complex but will include in some cases the ties of kinship and love and perhaps a dependence on the abuser for essential support. Additionally, there may be a lack of realistic alternatives for the individual to choose between. The options may seem to consist of a choice between risking further abuse and accepting a placement in an institution. There are limited legal powers to overrule the wishes of a competent older person and to enforce protection on that person who has experienced (or continues to experience) abuse even if the abuser could be subject to prosecution. Older people are adults with full citizenship rights, and the right to autonomy and self-determination, from both legal and moral perspectives, should remain of paramount importance in considerations of abuse and neglect.

The most problematic area for professionals who deal with such situations has been where there is doubt as to the older person's mental competence and their decision-making capacity. This dilemma has been encountered in the area of professional practice for many years but was not considered in a legalistic framework until it was addressed by a series of papers from the Law Commission (1991, 1993a, b, c, 1995). The overall remit of the Law Commission was to consider issues concerning decision making and mentally incapacitated adults, not exclusively older people but obviously encompassing situations in which older people might be in need of support and assistance in terms of decision making, if not protection.

In 1995, the Law Commission published a report that was laid before Parliament, containing proposals, in draft form, for a piece of legislation. One of the principal recommendations made was for 'authorised officers' to have rights of entry to a situation of suspected abuse and the capacity to obtain an emergency assessment order to adequately investigate difficult circumstances. The maintenance of personal autonomy is stressed throughout the Law Commission proposals, including the final report, leaving as much decision making with the individual as possible.

If mental competence is not at issue, the full right to self-determination should remain. The Law Commission paid particular attention to the fact that, in order to preserve the dignity and independence of the individual as far as possible, a decision that might be considered to be eccentric or contrary to the judgement of the professional should not be open to challenge on these grounds alone. To date the proposals have not been enacted but it is possible that legislation will be forthcoming during the lifetime of the Labour administration that came to power in May 1997.

The concept of duty to care is a further area of notable contrast when the situations of children and dependent older people are compared. In current society, there is an obligation on parents to care for their children. This includes the need to protect children when necessary, and abuse is therefore considered as a failure to carry out the caring task, in particular in relation to the provision of protection. If the parent is the perpetrator of the abuse, there may be additional concern for the safety of any other children in terms of the parent's capacity to provide adequate care and a safe environment. With regard to the care of physically and/or mentally dependent older people by family members there is no similar concept that is socially accepted. However, although there is no actual duty to care in the UK, there may be the perception by individual family members of a societal pressure and moral obligation to do so.

The concept of responsibility for older adults does not extend to the same total care expected for children. However, if a person assumes the role of carer for an adult, the concept of duty of care comes into effect from that point. There is an additional assumption by the general public that the state has a key role in the provision of care for this sector of the population (Diba, 1996). It is of course rather ironic that if the state *does* have a major role in the provision of care for older adults, there may also be 'societal abuse' by the state as evidenced by the limited and underfunded services from both health and social care.

There is a further problem in developing indicators of elder abuse in relation to domestic violence occurring in old age. Some such situations may be of many years' duration and continue in later life; others may arise in old age (for further detail, see Kingston and Penhale, 1995). Ogg suggests that it is possible to distinguish situations in which abuse is linked to issues of gender and power in interpersonal relationships from those where the abuse results from dependence and vulnerability due to disability (Ogg, 1993). However, there is also an acknowledgement of the need for further work, including research, in this area, as it seems that this distinction has previously been somewhat unclear and also because situations can occur where a combination of both types of abusive situations exist and interact.

Methodological problems arise, too, for the following reasons. Many of the studies that have taken place consist of small, unrepresentative samples of cases known to an agency or organisation. There has often been a lack of any standard definition of abuse used in such studies – most of which have employed different methodologies, including different techniques for sampling, data collection and analysis. There has also been a lack of studies using case–control methods, with a few notable exceptions (see Bennett et al, 1997). Some studies have been of an exploratory nature, with surveys and questionnaires designed for that particular piece of research. Additionally, there have been very few attempts to replicate some of the more reputable studies cross-culturally. It is therefore very difficult to compare adequately the findings from the studies that have taken place, or to generalise from them. This also means that it is extremely hard to resolve such issues as the incidence and prevalence of abuse, causal factors and identifying who is most at risk of abuse.

Professionals also experience a range of difficulties in both recognising and responding to abuse. This situation is exacerbated by methodological difficulties such as those already outlined. What must also be taken into account, however, is that the whole topic of abuse is a highly emotive and sensitive issue which many individuals, including professionals, do not wish to acknowledge. Many older people often deny the existence of any mistreatment and indeed may have their own strategies for resolving their own problem. It is therefore strongly suspected that the number of known cases represents but a small proportion of the total.

It is hard to quantify the prevalence of elder abuse. Current estimates are low, and research into this area is problematic for reasons already stated. The assumption of a low rate of prevalence might mean that professionals tackle cases of abuse only rarely. This presupposes, of course, that they are recognised by the professional as cases of abuse at all!

Ethical issues

There are important ethical issues in research into elder abuse, encompassing such factors as disclosure and confidentiality. This is partly due to the sensitivity of researching interpersonal violence in general. Questions such as the following arise when planning research in this area.

- What should a researcher do if, during their research, there is a disclosure of abuse?
- How far should confidentiality of an individual be maintained if a disclosure is made during the course of the research?
- Are there any circumstances in which confidentiality will be breached?
- Are there any differences in approach if the disclosure relates to a third party rather than to the individual?

In order to safeguard the interests of the individuals participating in the research and also the researchers involved, a protocol encompassing these factors must be established before the research starts. In addition, the researchers require sensitivity to the complexities of abuse and should be skilled in asking questions of participants in a way that is neither inquisitorial nor voyeuristic. Clearly this also extends to the use in research projects of interviewers, who must also be appropriately trained and prepared to deal with potential disclosures and issues related to confidentiality. Any research proposal should address such issues at the proposal stage, and mechanisms must be developed to deal appropriately with them.

The issue of ethics committees has caused some concern for researchers in recent years. All health-related research involving human subjects must have the approval of a properly constituted ethics committee. Increasingly this requirement is extending into the domain of social care. The principal task of an ethics committee is to assess every aspect of the proposed research process so that everyone is assured that the research is not only justified but also accords with ethical principles. The committee has to be convinced that important areas in the research process are adhered to.

The first main area is that of informed consent. This means that the nature of the research must be explained to potential participants in straightforward language and that all the potential risks (if any) arising from the research are outlined. The explanation should include details of any procedure to be used and/or any questions to be asked, indicating if these might touch on sensitive or personal areas. The potential participant must understand the explanation and must have the right to refuse to take part (or be able to withdraw from the research at any point in the process). This must be fully explained to the person from the point of initial contact, and if necessary repeated later; this would be the case, for example, if interviews were taking place with the same individuals at different points in time. Individuals can thus refuse to participate in any research if they consider that their physical or mental well-being could be compromised. In medical terms this refusal should not place the person in any jeopardy as to their status with regard to any further treatment. A further key principle is that individuals must not be pressured into agreeing to participate in the research. However, it may be slightly problematic for researchers to indicate beforehand the types of questions to be asked during the research, as this might have the effect of deterring individuals from agreeing to participate.

In broad terms the existence of such procedures means that only mentally competent individuals can give consent (usually both in writing and verbally) to participate in a study or piece of research. Generally, therefore, the majority of mentally frail people, whom many believe comprise one of the groups most vulnerable to abuse, are excluded from participation on the grounds that they are unable to give informed consent. This is viewed as a major methodological weakness in research that uses either self-disclosure or victimisation surveys. This is not to say that such surveys do not need to be conducted, but future research will have to consider more fully, perhaps by the use of more in-depth qualitative interviews, questions regarding the process of abuse. It has been suggested that research involving both 'victims' and 'perpetrators' is necessary, but that it should take place where the conflict has been resolved and is not ongoing (Ogg, 1993).

The second major principle is that of confidentiality. This principle is fundamental to all research work, especially in the fields of health and social care, but is particularly important when dealing with a sensitive and emotive topic such as abuse. The major dilemma that has been identified, however, relates to the questions indicated above. What should happen if, during a research interview, the client discloses severe and possibly life-threatening abuse but does not wish the researcher to break confidentiality? Is it legitimate for the researcher to allow a serious crime to continue, even to the point of murder? If this course of action is not correct, to whom is the researcher to disclose and break confidentiality? Such complex areas as these are not yet resolved in any formal sense, nor are there nationally agreed guidelines as to how to proceed in such situations. Currently, therefore, each group of researchers wishing to conduct a research project has to arrive at a bespoke agreement with the local ethics committee if the project is to involve patients.

The design of research projects is influenced by ethical considerations such as those already outlined. There are also organisational and social constraints that arise from the nature of the research itself. It would seem that our understanding of elder abuse and neglect is at least partly determined by the nature of the questions that research projects set out to answer and the methodological and ethical constraints within which projects are conducted. The methodological and ethical issues that arise from the unique nature of elder abuse research should be stated clearly in the final report, because they influence the design of research projects and also affect the way that the research is finally reported (Ogg, 1993).

Two further areas need to be considered in researching abuse and neglect. The first of these concerns finance. Interpersonal violence and neglect are not popular or 'hot' issues. There is no queue of potential funders waiting to give money to researchers keen to explore the issues more fully. This to some extent explains why much of the research that has been done has been small scale and somewhat limited. To date there has been no large-scale research funded to investigate this area; indeed the future of research into elder abuse and neglect does not look set to alter. This obviously deters some researchers and also adds to the general difficulty in research terms. The second area relates to the nature of the research itself. As already emphasised, this is a complex and sensitive area in which to work. Researchers will undoubtedly need adequate support and de-briefing systems for themselves when dealing in some depth with potentially distressing incidents. This aspect should be fully taken into account in the design of studies into abuse and neglect.

Research findings

Since the early 1990s there have been an increasing number of studies in elder abuse and neglect, both in the UK and elsewhere. A comprehensive review of the research that has taken place is not possible in this book. What *is* provided here is a summary of what may be considered to be major pieces of research from a number of different countries, which have added to our knowledge base about the topic.

The research being performed in the Scandinavian countries, together with the creation of the government-funded Resource and Research Centre on Family Violence in Norway, makes these countries one of the most influential areas in Europe working on elder abuse. The countries are considered in turn.

Finland

The earliest reports of elder abuse in Finland date back to the mid-1980s: shelters to help younger women who had been subject to domestic violence were contacted by older women in need of similar assistance (Heinanen, 1986). A more recent study of 1,086 older people living in private dwellings in a semi-industrialised town in Finland, conducted to explore the extent of the problem, suggested a prevalence rate of 5 per cent of people aged 65 years and older experiencing elder abuse (Kivelä et al, 1992). This same research identified poor health, depression, loneliness and a low level of life satisfaction among the victims of abuse. The abusers were mostly spouses, adult children or other close relatives with poor family relationships.

Sweden

The Swedish context of elder abuse has been very well summarised (Saveman, 1994). The principal report examines research findings obtained between 1985 and 1991. Research has identified awareness about elder abuse and knowledge of actual cases (Tornstam, 1989). The abuse of older people with dementia by informal carers has also been recognised through research (Grafström et al, 1992).

In a study aimed at determining patterns of abuse of older people living in their own homes in one county in Sweden, 12 per cent of district nurses reported 30 cases (Saveman et al, 1993). Half of the victims had a disturbed mental state; the abuser was most commonly a relative. The most frequent form of abuse reported was psychological abuse. An article about a further study described cases of elder abuse reported by home care service personnel across Sweden (Saveman and Nordberg, 1993). The article also included information on the type of intervention offered and opinions on additional intervention strategies. In all, 97 cases of abuse were reported; the majority of victims were female. Many of those abused were physically or psychologically disabled; the abuser was most commonly either the spouse or an adult child. Psychological abuse and financial exploitation were the most common forms of abuse encountered. In 75 per cent of cases intervention was offered to assist the situation.

Norway

The research focus in Norway has concentrated on family conflict and was initially investigated by an anthropologist with research colleagues (Johns et al, 1991). The overall prevalence figure, which was obtained from a pilot project in a community in Oslo, was 2.5 per cent (Johns, 1993). It has been suggested that the lack of knowledge and training of professionals about these issues has been a major problem. There are reports of repeated approaches to agencies by individuals which often seem to result only in a further referral to another service. This is perceived by victims and their families as rejection, several using the expression, 'I met the wall' (Hydle and Johns, 1992). The Ministry of Social Affairs has recognised that there is a problem, and has provided some government funds for initiatives at the complementary levels of research and policy development. Recent developments include the establishment in 1995 of a National Resource Centre for Information and Studies on Violence, with a major programme of work planned that has specific reference to elder abuse.

The Netherlands

There has also been a significant amount of research in the Netherlands relating to abuse. One report focuses on the results of an action project that set up two centres in one area of the country for a two-year period to raise awareness about elder abuse and to become centres for reporting cases (van Weeghel and Faber, 1995).

Both centres were established within existing care organisations, to allow for maximum liaison and appropriate care input. In addition, two separate models of intervention used in the different centres were assessed. These models were to provide extra care or increased use of the police/judicial systems.

Over the two-year period of the study the centres received 193 reports involving 197 suspected victims of abuse. Analysis of those cases revealed that 70 per cent of reporting came directly to the centre and 30 per cent were referred by care or service organisations. Of 51 older people who presented personally, only 1 met the centres' definition of elder abuse. Family members made 19 per cent of reports; GPs reported only 2 cases. Care providers (including district nurses, social workers and psychiatric nurses) were the most frequent reporters where the centre was based in the district home nursing service). In the area where the project was housed in a victim support centre, 9 cases were reported via the police, victim support centres and by telephone help services.

The most commonly reported forms of abuse were psychological abuse (67 per cent), followed by physical abuse (44 per cent), financial exploitation (41 per cent) and neglect (22 per cent). Violation of civil rights (such as confinement) occurred in 9 per cent of cases. There were no reports of sexual abuse made to either project centre.

The majority of victims were people over 75 years of age, most of whom were women (79 per cent). The victims lived with a partner in 22 per cent of cases or with a family member in 39 per cent of cases. The majority of abusers were men (80 per cent of cases). These were usually close relatives: a partner in 19 per cent of cases; a son, brother or other relative in 65 per cent. The researchers also analysed the characteristics of the victims, the abusers and the living situations. Victim characteristics were reported as vulnerability due to illness, disability or age. Abuser characteristics included addiction, criminality and abnormal psychological states as well as financial/economic difficulties. The living situation encompassed emotional dependence (the nature of the relationship, loyalty), the social network (as observed, significant others) and cultural values including the concepts of older people and ageism.

The final report from van Weeghel and Faber (1995) also provides information on how the centres publicised their work, the identified lack of support from GPs, the differences between the centres and how cases were handled as well as making specific recommendations.

Other research that has taken place in the Netherlands concerns dementia and abuse (Pot et al, 1996) and, more recently, the role of psychological aspects such as personality traits and coping styles in the development and perpetuation of abuse (Commijs, 1997).

The study concerning the possible links between dementia and elder abuse is worthy of further discussion. This study found high levels of verbal aggression (30.2 per cent of carers stated they had been verbally aggressive) whilst 10.7 per cent of responding carers reported that they had been physically aggressive towards the person with dementia whom they cared for (Pot et al, 1996). Both types of aggression seemed to be related to living in the same household as the person they were caring for and caring for a male. Furthermore, both types were positively related to caring for an elderly person with higher levels of cognitive impairment and physical dependence. In addition, verbal aggression seemed to be associated with providing higher levels of care, whereas physical aggression appeared to be more related to a higher level of 'psychological complaints' affecting the carer (the study forming part of a longitudinal study of the psychological complaints of informal carers of people with dementia).

This study aimed to compare the situations of carers who reported verbal aggression with those who reported physical aggression. (The rationale given for using the term 'aggression' rather than 'abuse' was to avoid the negative and criminal connotations of 'abuse' and also to look at behaviours irrespective of either the consequences for the person being cared for or the underlying intent of the carer.) This is nevertheless a useful and important study because it was the first to attempt a comparative study of carers of older people with dementia who act abusively towards them. It also specifically considered abuse against people diagnosed as having dementia.

The comparative element of the study considered differences between carers in relation to a number of factors: demographics (of carers and of people with dementia); the psychological complaints of the carer; and characteristics of the care recipient. The psychological complaints were assessed with standard screening tools adapted for use in the Netherlands. The study determined that physical aggression differed from verbal aggression in a number of ways and should not therefore be considered as just an extension of verbal aggression. Different intervention strategies seemed to be necessary, for example attempting to reduce the psychological complaints of the carer and the amount of 'burnout' in situations of physical aggression. Further studies that replicate such findings from different cultural perspectives would clearly be of value. In particular, a consideration of what might assist in the resolution of such situations will be beneficial.

Australia

In Australia recognition of the existence of elder abuse has led to a number of published studies from different states (New South Wales: Kurrle et al, 1991, 1992, 1993a; Victoria: Barron et al, 1990; South Australia: McCallum et al, 1990). In April 1993 the Federal Minister for Community Services authorised the formation of a Working Party on the Protection of Older People as a way for the country as a whole to address the issue.

In an article containing case reports, the annual rate of referrals to a Geriatric and Rehabilitation Service concerning elder abuse was 4.6 per cent (Kurrle, 1993a). Increasing the levels of awareness and knowledge about the problem among medical practitioners was determined as a priority.

In Adelaide a small-scale study attempted to define the range of problems encountered by professional service workers in an urban setting (McCallum, 1990). If the 4.6 per cent rate given above is adjusted for the total population, including older people in institutions, this gives an overall incidence of about 3 cases per 1,000 population (McCallum, 1993). It was suggested that the term 'elder abuse' should be abandoned and that policies should be developed to deal with a range of situations including neglect, domestic violence, conflict and financial exploitation. The key objective here was to develop a number of different services corresponding to different types of abuse (McDermott, 1993).

Intervention strategies that have been developed in Australia include local models (Barron et al, 1990) and a major input from the Carers Association. It has produced a Carer Support Kit, which includes information and aids such as a stress reduction tape for carers. There has also been some research concerning dementia and elder abuse. A study by Kurrle and colleagues determined that, in their sample, 46 per cent of those who had been abused had a significant level of dementing illness (ie moderate to severe confusion), whilst some 65 per cent had major physical disabilities or chronic health problems (Kurrle et al, 1992). A further study of importance is that reported by Sadler and colleagues (1995), which took place in the same region of Australia as that of Kurrle. This study attempted a case–control methodology (considered more reliable in research terms) and reported on 54 cases of abuse and 100 people with dementia who had not been abused. All of the individuals studied were clients of a particular rehabilitation and aged care service. The study seemed to confirm the existence of a strong link between dementia and elder abuse.

When dementia was present with other predisposing factors, such as substance abuse or psychiatric illness on the part of the carer or pre-existing family conflict, there was a significant risk of abuse happening. The mere presence of dementia, even with the existence of disturbed and aggressive behaviour on the part of the person with dementia, did not seem to result in a higher risk of either psychological or physical abuse for that person. However, carers themselves seem to be at risk of physical and/or psychological abuse (Sadler et al, 1995).

A review article concerning developments in recognition of the need for a response to elder abuse in Australia indicated variations in the nature and progress of responses between the states and territories (Kurrle, 1993c). This was thought to reflect the differing nature and structure of relevant services. The article presented an overview of the ways in which the issues had been dealt with at research, community and government levels. This included each state and territory and also the work of the Commonwealth Office for the Aged for the whole country.

The first part of the article reported on clinical cases and interventions (Kurrle, 1993b). The interventions used and outcomes achieved were reviewed in a follow-up study of 54 cases of abuse identified in a one-year study of a population using 'aged care services'. The article indicated that such intervention strategies as counselling, community services and respite care were initially successful. In a few cases the situation was resolved and the client remained at home. There were some cases of continuing abuse in which the client chose to stay in the abusive situation and relationship. In most cases, however, the outcome in the longer term was institutionalisation. This last outcome was reported as illustrating the need to separate victim and abuser to completely resolve the situation, and simultaneously pointing to the high levels of disability and dependency in the population studied, given the high-need admission criteria to such institutions (Kurrle, 1993b).

The results of this study (Kurrle, 1993b) allowed the author to construct two comparative tables: one indicated how different types of abuse seem to be related to different causes; the second examined the link between the different causes of abuse and specific intervention strategies for them. For example, one strategy is to use alternative accommodation, respite care, community care services or guardianship where the abuse seems to be related to the dependency of the victim.

United Kingdom

Research into elder abuse in the UK has been limited but fairly consistent. From quite modest beginnings in the late 1980s there has been a steady stream of relatively small-scale studies of different aspects of abuse. One study considered the likely prevalence of abuse as part of a wider household survey (Ogg and Bennett, 1992). This determined that the prevalence of psychological abuse was 5 per cent, whilst financial abuse and physical abuse were 2 per cent each. There has not been any replication of this study, and attempts to conduct large-scale studies of such aspects as risk factors (an attempt to repeat North American work in order to see if the findings are relevant in the UK) have not received funding support.

Some research examining the role of education in professional training (Kingston et al, 1995; McCreadie et al, 1998) established the importance of the inclusion of the topic of elder abuse in curricula for professional training and for ongoing training for qualified professionals. There has also been some consideration of financial matters (Rowe et al, 1993; Troke, 1994) and a pan-European project concerning abuse in residential care (Beneito et al, 1997). The role of dementia in abusive situations has been addressed by several studies (Cooney and Mortimer, 1995; Compton et al, 1997).

Homer and Gilleard, in their study of a population that had regular respite care from a geriatric service, reported that 45 per cent of carers indicated that they had abused their relative. Of this 45 per cent, some 14 per cent admitted to physical abuse. The study found that violence (or threat of violence) by the person with dementia seemed to lead to a violent response by the carer (Homer and Gilleard, 1990). This led to the suggestion by the researchers that it was disturbed and disruptive behaviour by the care recipient that was likely to result in abuse by the carer, rather than simply the presence of cognitive impairment such as dementia. A recent small-scale study of 38 carers in Northern Ireland seems to echo this finding, as the factors of significance in abusive situations were poor relationships before the onset of disease, abuse (physical or verbal) or problem behaviours by the person being cared for and the poor health of the carer (Compton et al, 1997). In this study, 34 per cent of the carers admitted to verbal abuse and 10 per cent admitted to physical abuse.

The finding that carers who reported being physically abusive to the person they cared for were more likely to report abuse (of themselves) by that person has also been duplicated in studies published by Coyne and colleagues in North America in 1993 and by Sadler and colleagues in Australia in 1995. This suggests a degree of consistency despite cultural variability and different populations being studied. One interpretation is that abusive or aggressive behaviour by a person who is cognitively impaired is a risk factor for the development and perpetuation of abusive situations. Further research would assist in determining whether this finding holds across other cultures (eg in less developed countries or in the Far East) and whether there are any other variables of significance that need to be taken into account.

The effectiveness of particular types of intervention has also been considered in a small number of studies. A study of a group of carers using an in-patient respite care facility in south London did not find any particular increase in dependency among couples who were abusive as compared with non-abusive carers and their dependants (Homer and Gilleard, 1994). Seventy-seven carers and the older people they cared for were interviewed separately. There was no observable improvement in the carers' emotional well-being as a whole, although the functional ability and social behaviour of some of the patients improved. In this group of 77 carers, 35 admitted to verbal abuse, 11 to physical abuse and 8 to neglect of the person whom they cared for.

Both carers and care recipients were asked if they would like additional respite care, or a different sort of respite care. Compared with the control group of carers (who did not admit to abuse), there was no significant increase in demand for respite care, nor was it seen as more valuable by the carers or care recipients who were in abusive relationships. This held true also for the small number of care recipients who were involved in abuse of their carers.

A substantial amount of work has been done on the development of policies and procedures in statutory organisations. In the most recent of these, the voluntary organisation Action on Elder Abuse conducted a survey of all health trusts, health authorities (purchasers) and social services departments in England and Wales to ascertain their policies and procedures (Action on Elder Abuse, 1995). Action on Elder Abuse has also produced an annotated bibliography of research taking place in the UK (McCreadie, 1995). An excellent report detailing the research findings from a number of different countries and considering different domains, including research developments and future directions, was produced in 1996 (McCreadie, 1996). This provides a comprehensive review of the research field and findings, and may well be of further interest to the reader.

Messages from research

In 1995, the Department of Health produced a seminal document entitled *Child Protection: Messages from research*. This major publication was concerned with the dissemination of research findings in relation to child abuse and child protection, in particular detailing the results from research that had been commissioned and funded by the Department of Health. As has been evidenced throughout this chapter, we are far from having an equivalent document in relation to elder abuse.

Until the 1990s, successive UK governments had neither funded nor commissioned research in elder abuse, although the production of McCreadie's report in 1996 testifies to growing official acknowledgement of the problem. This relative neglect has resulted in a situation in which researchers have tended to conduct small-scale studies of specific areas, such as professional education, which either do not require external funding or have already obtained small amounts of funding. In many respects this is no different from the situation elsewhere, although in the USA there has been some government support of initiatives and funding of programmes through legislation such as the Older Americans Act (1987 Amendment). Because of the lack of any national framework with regard to elder abuse, such developments as have occurred have been somewhat piecemeal and ad hoc.

Research that has been undertaken has thus remained largely small scale and locally based, and the methodological problems outlined at the beginning of this chapter continue, therefore, to be reproduced by such approaches. This is not to say that all research except that employing more reliable methodologies such as case–control techniques and large samples should cease, but it is apparent that what is needed is the development of a coherent strategy and approach to the development of research, intervention and prevention in this whole area. A nationally agreed programme of research and development in elder abuse, as occurred in the arena of child protection, would clearly assist in this regard. Clearly, the funding of larger scale research projects is a concomitant of this, for without funding it will not be possible to conduct larger scale projects. This could perhaps be usefully achieved within the broader framework of a fuller exploration of the abuse of vulnerable adults.

It is important, however, that practitioners guard against any tendency to develop assumptions with regard to elder abuse. This is precisely because the knowledge base about the topic is so limited at present. A number of practice-related documents have been produced for practitioners (usually in the form of procedures to be followed), which include checklists of indicators of abuse and risk factors involved. Many of these have not been substantiated by research, and caution should be exercised in adhering too rigidly to them.

Nevertheless, the research indicates that certain individuals do seem more likely to be abused than others. There are clear differences in terms of gender and also the risk of abuse to individuals who are cognitively impaired, although the reasons for these differences are not yet fully clear. Practitioners need to be aware of such factors and take them into account when assessing abusive situations and working with individuals to resolve them. As highlighted earlier in this chapter, practitioners must also pay due regard to the existing legal situation and the boundaries of individual freedom and choice. The balance between protection, autonomy and self-determination is a fine one, and people working in such situations must apply knowledge gained from the work of such organisations as the Law Commission.

There are a number of possible directions for future research in this area, some of which relate to the themes discussed in this chapter (eg the need for research to be ethically sound). Whilst not wishing to be prescriptive about the areas to be covered, particularly in the absence of any nationally agreed framework, McCreadie (1996) has identified two main priorities for research. First, as already suggested in this chapter, there is clearly a need to be as rigorous in methodological terms as possible, and to pay attention to the quality of any research undertaken. Secondly, there is a pressing need to examine different types of abuse, including multiple forms of abuse, and to try to discover why some individuals (women, people with dementia or other types of ill-health) are more likely to experience abuse.

Research in these areas might usefully consider abuse that affects other vulnerable groups of adults, for example those with problems relating to mental health or disability (McCreadie, 1996). It is necessary also to consider interventions further: to discover whether the procedures that are being produced by health and social care agencies and organisations are effective; what professionals actually do in practice (beyond the application of the procedure); and which interventions are effective for which types of abuse. Such an approach would probably require the development of action research projects that would then be evaluated with a focus on the outcomes of the interventions used. Additionally, further investigation of the settings in which abuse occurs would prove useful, as would more detailed examination of issues of gender, power and ethnicity in abusive situations.

The above list may appear lengthy and have the air of a 'wish-list'. It may also seem defeatist to state that we are still a long way from being able to produce a document equivalent to *Child Protection: Messages from research*. Much has been achieved in the last decade; much more will be achieved in the years to come. We know more about elder abuse now than we did, and each piece of the jigsaw needs to be fitted with precision and care. We know something of the prevalence; we know that certain individuals are more likely to be abused; we also know, a little, about potential risk factors (although they have not yet been verified as applicable in the UK). As McCreadie astutely observed: 'Research will continue to be indispensable in providing the necessary knowledge base' (McCreadie, 1996, p 111).

It is this knowledge base that will provide the substantive foundation on which appropriate policies and responses to the problem can be developed. It is perhaps, above all, an indication of the complexity of this whole topic that we still seem in many respects to be at the beginning of the journey.

Acknowledgement

The author acknowledges with thanks the assistance of Gerry Bennett and Paul Kingston in preparing this chapter.

chapter 2

Putting elder abuse on the agenda: achievements of a campaign

Jill Manthorpe

This chapter takes a reflective look at the policy dimension of elder abuse. In doing so it employs some of the ideas about policy that have been highly influential in developing understanding of the policy process as it affects elder abuse internationally and, more specifically, in the UK. It starts with a discussion of the role of individuals and organisations, noting that there are important alliances and continuities. The work of Action on Elder Abuse is used to illustrate some of these threads. The chapter ends with an appreciation of the achievements of the loosely constructed campaign concerning elder abuse and observations about some of its omissions and problematic areas.

The Lone Crusader?

In 1984 Age Concern England, the voluntary organisation working with older people, produced a seminal work, *Old Age Abuse* (Eastman, 1984), greatly revised in a second edition (Eastman, 1994). Eastman's position was important in straddling the divide between practitioners (he is an experienced social worker) and managers (he is currently director of a social services department). In being published for a professional rather than an academic audience, the book had a wide impact.

Eastman emphasised that he was not engaged in the production of 'research' though he employed a series of case histories taken from his own records or from letters he had received (Eastman, 1984, p 6). This disclaimer that the work was not research does of course depend on one's definition of research but his contribution was to place old age abuse in the context of the then largely neglected informal care sector where he argued that caring relationships had the potential to break down. Eastman described his aim as informing welfare professionals of the possibility of abuse existing 'on a scale hitherto unknown or even acknowledged by professionals, the media, and society as a whole' (p 11). The written or electronic word has great durability and dominates historical accounts, so it is important to note that Eastman also played (and continues to do so) a major role in publicising elder abuse through conference presentations. In the foreword to *Old Age Abuse*, Hobman observed that Eastman's contribution had been a 'catalyst' in raising the profile of the subject (p 7).

Eastman's role was unique: his findings were derived from practice (his own and others) and he has remained interested in the subject throughout his subsequent managerial career. His thinking has developed around the subject: for example, in the first edition of *Old Age Abuse* he discussed the many unresolved problems with the relationships between power, dependency and abuse. In the second edition he balanced the former's concentration on domestic abuse by including residential or institutional manifestations of abuse. In choosing to edit a collection of 16 chapters written by others for the second edition of *Old Age Abuse*, Eastman encompassed a wide range and illustrated the extent to which, in ten years, thinking had developed. A year earlier Decalmer and Glendenning (1993) had produced a collection of ten chapters, largely revised in a second edition in 1997. The pioneering period 1980–1984 was thus succeeded by a proliferation of publications, particularly from 1993 until the present.

Campaigning developments

Other authors, while acknowledging Eastman's role, place it in the context of the work of the voluntary sector, noting that the 'surge of interest' in abuse from the early 1980s was 'largely spearheaded by the voluntary organisation Age Concern' (Penhale and Kingston, 1995, p 223). They cite Cloke's (1983) review of the literature, together with Eastman's book (1984), as evidence of Age Concern's interest, given that Age Concern was the publisher in both cases.

To this growing list of contributions should be added the report *The Law and Vulnerable Elderly People* (Age Concern England, 1986), which specifically addressed old age abuse as an issue composed of multiple dilemmas about consent, intervention, autonomy and representation. This report was one of the earliest works in the UK to think constructively about the issue of abuse. It was also the product of a multi-professional and multi-interest debate that sought to develop a consensus model for legal and procedural change. Many points of the report presage current debates about elder abuse: notably its discussion of 'whistle-blowing', of police checks of criminal histories among care staff or volunteers, of the ad hoc response to incidents from local authorities and of a lack of 'systematic procedures and uniform national guidance' (p 32).

Whilst *The Law and Vulnerable Elderly People* is not always included in chronologies charting the development of thinking about elder abuse, it is possible to see it as part of Age Concern's sustained interest in the subject and its strategy to work for legal reform. Age Concern's *National Policy* (1991) is divided into separate sections covering vulnerable older people and the law (para 6.7) and old age abuse (para 6.8) but clearly there are many interrelated aspects. What is notable from Age Concern, however, is the degree of concentration on policy – in many ways the converse of the academic debate that has striven for more clarity in other areas, notably definitions, theoretical frameworks and risk factors. It may be helpful to outline briefly Age Concern's policy on this issue (established in 1991) to set a marker for the debates about the 1980s. It calls for guidelines (multi-agency), for the identification of people at risk, for action when abuse is suspected, for co-ordinated and multi-disciplinary policies and training, and finally for systematic research into 'the causes, extent, identification and treatment of people who are involved in abusing situations' (para 6.8.5). In 1990, Age Concern England had convened a group of interested organisations to carry forward this policy agenda to work on guidelines for action that could be used across a wide range of settings (Age Concern et al, undated).

Policy system

There is little research into the formulation of policy among not-for-profit organisations, at either national or local level. Attention is focused on policy making at government level, despite the immense contribution to national social welfare by the voluntary sector, particularly in the nineteenth century (see Kearns, 1997). How the voluntary sector decides its own policy in contemporary Britain is far less clear, and the study of elder abuse itself may have an important role in establishing appropriate procedures.

At one level we can identify the importance of personal biographies and commitment. Eastman, with his ability to write and appeal to his professional peers while involving a wider constituency of those involved with older people's welfare, was clearly a 'catalyst'. However, those within Age Concern, such as its current (then Deputy) Director, Sally Greengross, may also have provided a very receptive ear and supportive environment. As she observed in the preface to *The Law and Vulnerable Elderly People* (Age Concern England, 1986) her background in child protection played an influential role.

It is therefore helpful when charting the history of the understanding of elder abuse to see a set of interlocking wheels operating, affecting each other and wider social environments. Phillipson and Biggs (1995), for example, locate discussions of elder abuse in a broader community of interests about older people. Other writers, working from feminist perspectives, observe both the late recognition of elder abuse in 'gendered discourse' and the paucity of debate about the gender aspects of abuse among those focusing on elder abuse (eg Aitken and Griffin, 1996; Whittaker, 1997). These broad macro-perspectives should be related to more focused debates about the law, for example the decision of the Law Commission to investigate and report to Parliament on the legal standing of vulnerable and/or mentally incapacitated adults. The Law Commission's consultation documents (1991, 1993) and its report *Mental Incapacity* (1995) have been influential in identifying the proper balance between protection and empowerment and also in recommending a series of legal reforms, particularly concerning matters of finance, treatment and emergency protection (the 1993 Consultation Paper being extended to examine the position of mentally incapacitated and other vulnerable adults).

The level of national policy making was thus an important but not the only focus of attention for those interested in elder abuse. As described above, Age Concern noted early on that the decentralised model of social care and protection operating in the UK made it essential to campaign for guidelines across all, preferably multi-agency, authorities. Rather than identifying various short periods of time as 'rich' or 'fallow' in discussions of elder abuse in the 1980s and 1990s, it is probably more appropriate to identify some discrete but many more interconnected debates.

Action on Elder Abuse

From its inception, Action on Elder Abuse has been a national membership organisation (a registered charity) that aims 'to prevent abuse in old age by promoting changes in policy and practice through raising awareness, education, promoting research and the collection and dissemination of information' (publicity leaflet, undated). It describes itself as being founded by a group of health and social care professionals, academics and representatives of the voluntary sector. The prime 'movers and shakers' – Gerry Bennett, Paul Kingston and Bridget Penhale – had met in 1990 and established a multi-disciplinary steering group (their professional backgrounds were medicine, nursing and social work respectively) that received pump-priming finance from Age Concern England. The link with Age Concern was continued when Action on Elder Abuse was launched in 1993 as a subsidiary charity of

Age Concern England. The following year, a constitution was adopted, the first member of staff appointed and trustees elected. Core funding was applied for and received from the Department of Health.

The pattern of launching discrete, eventually separate, 'satellites' of Age Concern's work followed earlier successful examples in other areas (eg assisting with the precursor to the Pre-Retirement Association). Indeed Age Concern itself (with its former label of the National Old People's Welfare Council) had been a 'spin-off' from the National Council of Social Service (now the National Council for Voluntary Organisations). Age Concern, in a process of mutual adjustment, was able to give the benefit of its resources, expertise and patronage while Action on Elder Abuse was able to take forward swiftly an issue that seemed relevant to Age Concern's work and bringing it into contact with wider professional networks that were traditionally somewhat separate from Age Concern's main activities and image.

Action on Elder Abuse is an organisation that has grown quickly. In terms of the International Classification of Nonprofit Organisations (ICNPO) (see Davis Smith et al, 1995, pp 76–77) it fits into Group 7 as an organisation that works to protect or promote civil rights, to advocate the interests of a special constituency. However, it also provides services to the elderly (Group 4) and develops education, training and research (Group 2). Like many voluntary organisations, Action on Elder Abuse carries out a variety of functions and is active across a number of classifications, but in terms of the ICNPO classification its primary functions are located in Group 7 whereas Age Concern's work would be in Group 4. How far an organisation that receives major government funding can operate as a Group 7 (advocacy) organisation may be debatable but can be illustrated by the development of the Elder Abuse telephone helpline.

Elder abuse response

In 1995/6 Action on Elder Abuse ran a pilot national telephone helpline. During the year 550 callers were given information, and support where appropriate. The service was piloted in four varied local authority areas – Camden, Lewisham, Rochdale and Hampshire – with responses available also in Hindi, Urdu and Punjabi for the second half of the pilot. An evaluation of the pilot, *Hearing the Despair: The reality of elderly abuse* (Action on Elder Abuse and Family Policy Studies Centre, 1997), provided details of the service, as follows:

- nearly 60 per cent of calls were about specific incidents of abuse;
- trained volunteers were able to answer and respond to calls effectively but needed training and continued support to do so;
- representatives of local welfare agencies in the pilot areas observed an increase in interest in the subject.

Since November 1997 the Response Line has been operating as a national freephone helpline.

It is early days to comment on the impact of the Response Line and its role in the development of Action on Elder Abuse and understanding of elder abuse in the UK. However, initial observations suggest that there are a number of key features arising from the Response Line. First, elder abuse, like other subjects of public anxiety, is one in which individuals affected (in various ways) may seek advice from an 'expert', anonymised source of help. The nature of contact established through such helplines is complex: it is not simply a matter of reporting an incident but a dialogue between anonymous dislocated voices in which callers decide about the level and type of information they are willing to impart. As with other advice lines, the Response Line also serves as an information source for those involved in training and education: it is clear that many advice lines serve these wide ranges of functions.

The decision by Action on Elder Abuse (in which the present author took part) to establish a national helpline had the anticipated advantages of raising public awareness and, more specifically, of advising or supporting individuals with specific concerns. An example that has been placed in the public arena was the case of nurse Judith Jones who suspected sexual abuse of residents in the home where she worked. Her call to Action on Elder Abuse was referred to the organisation Public Concern at Work (see its annual report, 1997), which then gave expert advice about the collection of evidence. Mrs Jones was able to assist in the pursuit of a criminal charge, and the owner of the home was convicted of indecent assault and jailed for four years.

Such activity clearly fulfils a number of the stated objectives of Action of Elder Abuse – in particular providing guidance for the prevention of and action on the abuse of older people. Its financial support from the Department of Health is also effective because helplines are an accepted and visible response to a social problem.

For the Department of Health and Action on Elder Abuse the Response Line marks a happy unity of interest. A service is provided that meets the objectives of both in a relatively efficient manner because the employees of Action on Elder Abuse are few and their volunteers are inexpensive (although financial considerations are not uppermost for the latter). Other costs of Action on Elder Abuse are met by trusts or charities, thus removing the need for total governmental support and eliminating any implication that the government is paying the hand that bites it – if criticism of its activities ensues.

Social policy perspectives

Although much work has been done in seeking to identify and develop theoretical perspectives relevant to elder abuse, the policy context remains 'under-theorised'. Exceptionally, Biggs (1997) has analysed and demonstrated from a critical social perspective how the phenomenon of elder abuse has been shaped in professional and public understanding. He has located it, for example, in a debate about welfare rather than criminology and ascribes its lack of priority to implicitly ageist values. Moreover, Biggs has alluded to unconscious motivations and explanations for the perceptions of elder abuse – proposing that it reinforces images of older people as negative and second class (pp 86–87). Drawing on Foucault's ideas, he has suggested that policies and acceptance of the notion of elder abuse might serve to justify a policing and surveillance of care situations and later life in general.

However, it is the work of Blumer (1971) and Baumann (1989) that have been used more widely in policy analysis, most notably by Penhale and Kingston (1995, ch 9). Blumer's stages or phases of social policy construction are:

- emergence of a social problem;
- legitimisation of the problem;
- mobilisation of action;
- formation of an official action plan;
- implementation of the official plan (Blumer, 1971, p 226).

In the pages that follow, each phase is discussed in a way similar to the analysis conducted by Leroux and Petrunik (1990) of elder abuse as a social problem in Canada. Those authors were able to test the fit of the theory through research interviews, which is not attempted here.

Blumer's first stage, 'emergence', is seen less as a process by Penhale and Kingston than as a climate of concern about the problems of individual older people and their dependence on welfare systems. Such a 'problematisation' was also placed in the wider context of responses to family violence, problems of ageing and the perceived victimisation of elderly people in street crime.

This portrayal of 'emergence' as a rather diffuse and serendipitous process needs to take into account the way in which some issues come into the public domain while others are suppressed. Hugman (1995) has argued that 'as a new professionalism developed in services for older people there was less of an acceptance that "this is how it is" and a greater willingness to seek explanations for apparent injury or neglect' (p 495). In doing so he has developed an explanation of why abuse emerged as a sustained focus for professional and pressure group activity. In contrast to other issues, such as hypothermia, fuel costs or funeral payments, which were matters that were also articulated as social problems, the issue of elder abuse has emerged as a subject appropriate to the business of professionals, simultaneously prompting critical consideration of the latter's position in the welfare state generally.

Blumer's second phase of policy construction as the legitimisation of the problem was interpreted by Penhale and Kingston as the necessary bridge between professional interest in the subject and its acknowledgement by policy makers and the wider public. They observed that professional interest was not immediately or even belatedly shared by policy makers, far less by the general public. This was despite the very close links between professionals and Age Concern England who were often called upon to advise policy makers and other politicians (eg Law Commission, 1995, p 285). Levin (1997), however, has posited that, for policy makers to engage with an issue, they need to 'register' with a particular issue from a mass of other claims competing for attention. The process of registering is a matter of both perception and imperative: 'a feeling that impelled them to "do something" about that situation' (p 228). The combination of perception and imperative in Levin's view results in an interest in achieving an aim.

The notion of legitimisation, however, also requires agreements that the matter under consideration is a proper subject for policy attention: that it is acceptable for government or its agents to control in some way the activities of some of its citizens, or to protect those who do not want such assistance. This dilemma has been presented at several levels, with the control (through inspection, for instance) of those employed to care for older people being viewed as a more appropriate area for official intervention than the domestic sphere. It is perhaps not surprising that the division between abuse in domestic and in institutional locations still persists, as there is much broader acceptance that the institution is in some way a more public arena in which professionals have legitimate roles. For policy makers, reform or extra regulation of institutional care may be more acceptable territory.

Hogwood and Gurr (1984) also identified certain characteristics that might move an issue into a matter for action. These include perceptions that the issue is large scale, that it has an emotional content, and that it catches the public's imagination. Rather than locating these characteristics as being important in any single one of Blumer's stages, it is arguable that they apply cumulatively throughout all of them. In the case of elder abuse, professionals, academics and pressure groups have generally been extremely cautious about raising the emotional temperature. The ambiguities and tensions related to the issue of elder abuse mean that it is too simplistic to view it as a single issue.

Blumer's third developmental phase, the 'mobilisation of action', was considered by Penhale and Kingston (1995) as the stage most relevant to the UK context in the mid-1990s. At that time, they identified accelerating demands for government action. For example, sustained pressure was exerted by the newly formed group Action on Elder

Abuse and this attracted more and diverse media attention. In an apparent symbiotic relationship between pressure and policy, the then Junior Minister for Health, John Bowis, launched Action on Elder Abuse (partially funded by the Department of Health) with the express aim of policy development – or 'mobilisation', to use Blumer's phrase.

Blumer's stage of formation of an official action plan is clearly related to a discrete, self-contained social policy rather than a complex social issue or set of issues that relate to many interconnected governmental systems. At the time of writing, developments in the area of elder abuse are to be found in further consultation over the Law Commission's proposals, in revised regulation and inspection systems for residential care and in developments in family law reform. An action plan may have to be considered as a combination of incremental reforms rather than wholesale revision. At the level of agency purchasing and provision of health and social care, incremental processes also seem to have taken place, most social services departments now possessing the guidelines called for in the mid-1980s and spelled out in the practice guidelines issued by the Social Services Inspectorate/Department of Health (1993). Bennett and colleagues (1997) consider that the stage of 'official plan' has been reached in England and Wales. This may be true if we accept that an 'official plan' can be composed of a series of incremental measures, for in the UK there is as yet no consensus about what a broader plan might be. This means that we need to pay more attention to the connections between Blumer's phases and not simplify them into discrete stages with milestones that can be reached.

Blumer's model has particular appeal because it is linear and progressive. However, policy making and implementation are not linear. As Whitmore (1984) demonstrated in relation to child abuse, there are several levels of operation. Agencies, for example, have both their internal activities and inter-agency processes. Activities conducted by practitioners at the front line may not be entirely consistent with their agency's stated practice. Warnings need to be sounded about viewing all policy development as beneficial. Precisely because of the emotional, moral and value dimensions of abuse, there will be disagreement about what is acceptable and ethical.

Conclusion

Many reports on elder abuse pause to account or even apologise for its low priority and limited research base. It is possible, however, to argue that much has been achieved in a short period within the UK. There has, for example, been close collaboration among professionals at a time when much other research has pointed to difficulties in working together effectively (eg Manthorpe et al, 1996) in areas of community care for older people and to the sustained presence of professional stereotyping (Dalley, 1989). Whilst some might construe these arguments as self-seeking behaviour by professionals, the formation of joint guidelines, policies and procedures represents major practical achievements and a recognition of the potential contribution of different agencies and disciplines.

An associated achievement has been the practical demonstration of links between professionals, generally from the statutory sector, and the voluntary sector in the organisational forum of Action of Elder Abuse itself and its conferences and information or educational publications. In contrast to many events organised for a profession, or a sector of care, work on elder abuse is frequently characterised by a range of contributors and participants. At a time of competition between some sectors or agencies, this activity may have been helpful in providing holistic perspectives.

A third achievement is probably the pace of development which, as this chapter has illustrated, has been increasingly rapid. The development, moreover, has generally been without the notions of 'moral panic' that child protection workers and mental health practitioners may have found to be not particularly helpful. In taking forward a debate on a consensus model, it has clearly been important not to risk alienating care sector staff, for instance, or family carers or others who might easily be labelled 'typical abusers'. Achieving broad agreement in social policy is often a difficult task, for there are many interests to consider. It is perhaps significant that the debate about elder abuse has generally been characterised by a range of alliances – at times concerning specific aspects, but also in broad support.

It would be remiss to end this chapter on achievements without observations on problems or challenges. A key matter for those interested in elder abuse is to explore the perspectives of older people themselves and to pay due regard to their wishes and feelings. Engaging with organisations that represent older people on matters concerning pensions may be one way forward (see Ginn (1993) for a description of groups active in the UK). However, listening and responding to the views of older people is methodologically, ethically and practically fraught with problems: perhaps work needs to be more focused on what information professionals or pressure groups wish to acquire – and what they will do with it if it produces controversial results.

To what extent work on elder abuse has drawn on perspectives from other fields is of course difficult to quantify. Although many commentators have reflected on the connections and lessons learned from work in child protection, domestic violence and the abuse of other than elderly vulnerable adults, such links are constructed very much along welfare lines – the common factors being professional involvement, gender and powerlessness. New perspectives may help us determine the role of assumptions about ageing, ageism and the meaning of abuse.

This chapter has explored what is meant by putting elder abuse on the agenda. In terms of social policy the agenda is generally conceived to be that of policy makers, whereas, as we have noted, other groups have agendas that may give priority to other issues. It has also explored models of social policy construction and argued that a coherent 'policy' in respect of elder abuse may not square with the complexities and varied manifestations of abuse. What we understand by abuse plays a key role in determining how we view the relevance of policy and policy reform. To put elder abuse on the policy agenda might be an achievement but it is by no means a solution. More work on policy and its impact would seem highly appropriate because we are now at the stage where reforms should be evaluated.

Finally, on a personal note, the matters discussed in this chapter mirror the author's own professional thinking. One of the challenges of writing this chapter was to acknowledge and reflect on a personal perspective. Putting elder abuse on the agenda does not mean making it devoid of personal observations: one of the challenges for many of us who have been thinking about this subject for some time is how to reconcile professional or academic interests with political or personal commitments. Particularly promising in this connection are new interests in feminist approaches to issues of elder abuse (not simply in relation to violence), which may help to reconcile aspects that, otherwise, seem polarised.

chapter 3

Elder abuse as harm to older adults: the relevance of age

Phil Slater

In 1995, Collins Educational published a *Dictionary of Social Work* (Thomas and Pierson, 1995). The fact that this reference work included an entry for 'elder abuse' speaks volumes about the development of interest in, debate on and campaigning about the subject over the previous five years. Yet this would-be conferring of professional legitimacy cannot suppress the fact that the very phrase 'elder abuse' remains highly problematical. This was demonstrated by a particularly forceful article from Richard Hugman (1995), which asked why acts such as rape or robbery, normally regarded as simply criminal, should be redesignated as sexual or financial 'abuse' in the case of dependent elderly people. In other words, the term 'elder abuse' is over-inclusive. To redress this imbalance, Hugman proposed the concept of 'obligation of care', which serves to demarcate what ought to be two quite distinct discourses: criminality on the one hand, and health and welfare on the other. In this way, the meaning of 'elder abuse' would be slimmed down and sharpened up with reference to the specific 'abuse' component.

Problems remain, however, with 'elder', which implies an exclusive concern with older adults. To a great extent, of course, the specific age focus is explicitly deployed in the context of a critique of ageism as a social reality (Hughes, 1995; Manthorpe, 1997). Paradoxically, however, the age focus can unwittingly reinforce the uncritical, and fundamentally ageist, terminological segregation of 'elders', not as an oppressed sub-group within the broader concept of 'adults' but as an exclusive category distinguished from adults altogether. As a corollary to Hugman's critique of the over-inclusiveness of 'elder abuse', one might express this additional problem in terms of an under-inclusiveness of the separate concepts of 'adults at risk/vulnerable adults'.

This is obviously open to question. For example, in her foreword to a book on family violence across the life span (dealing in turn with child abuse, adult abuse and elder abuse), Olive Stevenson raised a now familiar question: 'is it "ageist" to separate out old people from other adults?' Wisely, she did not offer the false comfort of an undifferentiated yes or no. Instead, she pointed to the complexities and difficulties inherent in the subject: 'it is a minefield, conceptually and ethically' (Stevenson, 1995, p vii).

In line with this image, the present chapter hopes to fulfil something of a 'minesweeping' function. Commencing with an outline of the elder/adult debate, the chapter then attempts to separate out the frequently conflated sub-arguments of the protagonists, and to argue that a 'peaceful' synthesis of many of these arguments into a composite strategy is not only possible but already implied (though not yet explicitly articulated as such) in current developments. The unifying effect of the Law Commission's work on 'vulnerable adults' is seen as pivotal in this regard. Finally, to emphasise that the complexities of this strategy are not restricted to general questions of social policy and service management, the chapter concludes by teasing out the implications for direct practice.

Outlining the debate

When Age Concern published the first British book on what was then termed *Old Age Abuse* (Eastman, 1984), the age focus was assumed to be methodologically unproblematic: the idea of an alternative 'adult' focus was not even considered. Seven years later, when the Age Concern Institute of Gerontology published a modestly sub-titled 'exploratory study' on elder abuse, things had changed dramatically. Indeed, the author went so far as to assert that a lengthy debate on the meaning of 'elder abuse' would be futile, because 'a decision is first needed on whether to refer to adult abuse of which elder abuse is a part' (McCreadie, 1991, p 58).

What had transpired in the intervening years? First and foremost, the emerging North American elder/adult debate of the early 1980s had been recorded in scholarly books published on both sides of the Atlantic. A chapter destined to become a classic critique of the age-based focus of 'elder abuse' as inappropriate and actually ageist had been published by Stephen Crystal (1986). Equally classic defences of 'elder abuse' as a distinct category calling for special attention had been published by Finkelhor and Pillemer (1988) and Wolf and Pillemer (1989).

Of related significance were the parallel initiative on 'adults at risk' in response to the death of Beverley Lewis in the late 1980s (Association of Directors of Social Services, 1991) and the Law Commission's work on 'mental incapacitation', also commencing in the late 1980s and presented in overview form the same year (Law Commission, 1991). Neither of these developments was originally conceived as an overt challenge to the specific 'elder abuse' focus, but they inevitably prompted critical reflection, particularly when read in conjunction with the North American literature. By taking full cognisance of this complex terrain, and specifically highlighting the elder/adult question, the value of McCreadie's 'exploratory study' of 1991 can scarcely be over-stated.

Sadly, the effects thereof were not apparent in the first of the new wave of British books on elder abuse (Pritchard, 1992), but thereafter they were never off the agenda. One of two major books published the following year seriously considered the Crystal-style argument for a generic 'adults' focus, before unequivocally advocating the adoption of a model 'unique to elder abuse and neglect' (Bennett and Kingston, 1993, p 47). The other book, by contrast, presented the question of whether elder abuse has characteristics that distinguish it from the abuse of non-elderly adults as 'unresolved' (Decalmer and Glendenning, 1993, p 11).

A contributor to the second edition of Age Concern's 1984 classic went a step further by tentatively embracing the alternative 'adults' strategy (Eastman, 1994, ch 13). By contrast, a subsequent major publication on family violence across the life span, while acknowledging that elder abuse had similarities with other forms of domestic violence, reaffirmed Bennett and Kingston's view that 'a response should be based on the unique phenomena of elder abuse' (Kingston and Penhale, 1995, p 240).

Slowly but surely, this defence of an emerging orthodoxy against its critics had evolved into a counter-critique in its own right. One reads, for example, that 'having guidelines for "adults" makes the assumption that elderly people are no more at risk than members of the general population and could well lead to a failure of local authorities to address the special needs of elderly people who are at risk' (Decalmer and Glendenning, 1993, p 162). In turn, this riposte was subjected to a counter-counter-critique, charging the authors with factual inaccuracy, false logic and methodological incoherence (Slater, 1995).

In such a climate, it becomes all too easy for intellectual arguments to be affirmed or repudiated with primary, even instinctive, reference to their compatibility or otherwise with a campaigning 'cause'. As a result, complex sub-arguments may be unconsciously collapsed into one another, thereby seriously curtailing the scope for arriving at a differentiated judgement. If, by contrast, strategic considerations are to be pursued in earnest, the debate must first be broken down into its essential components.

Distilling the arguments

In the typology that follows, a global choice between 'elders' and 'adults' is transcended via the identification of four related but logically distinct dimensions to the age-specific question:

- *conceptual specificity* – clarifying the terms of reference of the problem;
- *legislative priority* – identifying a strategic objective for statutory reform;

- *policy targeting* – deciding on appropriate client groupings for overall operations;
- *service equitability* – promoting anti-ageist service delivery.

Spanning these four dimensions, a typology of arguments for and against the specific age focus can be constructed in the form of a set of representative arguments and counter-arguments. These are best understood as ideal-type abstractions from the live debate, as opposed to direct paraphrases let alone quotations: in this 'pure' form, none of the arguments can be said to be 'owned' by any particular participant in that debate. The citation of authors is intended solely as a convenient set of signposts to relevant reading, all of which wrestle with the complexities of the matter in hand and caution against intellectual rigidity.

Dimension I: Conceptual specificity

ARGUMENT

Elder abuse is a discrete phenomenon, displaying characteristics unique to old age in existing social structures, and requiring a specific professional response. (Wolf and Pillemer, 1989; Bennett and Kingston, 1993)

COUNTER-ARGUMENT

'Elder abuse' is a purely descriptive term indicating the age of the victim and should be subsumed under the broader analytical concept of adult abuse in the home/care setting. (Breckman and Adelman, 1988; Steinmetz, 1990)

Dimension II: Legislative priority

ARGUMENT

Specific protective legislation is required in recognition of the physical, mental and socially constructed vulnerabilities of old age. (Age Concern England, 1986; Stevenson, 1989)

COUNTER-ARGUMENT

Protective legislation should focus on individual capacity and circumstance, not on medical, psychiatric or sociological generalities. (Ashton, 1994; Law Commission, 1995)

Dimension III: Policy targeting

ARGUMENT

'Old age' is already differentiated as such in current social policy, which constitutes a positive basis for further developments. (Finkelhor and Pillemer, 1988; Ogg and Munn-Giddings, 1993)

COUNTER-ARGUMENT

The social policy construction of 'age' is reciprocally determined by ageist stereotyping, and should therefore be challenged and transcended. (Crystal, 1986; Scrutton, 1990)

Dimension IV: Service equitability

ARGUMENT

Failure to ring-fence specific 'elder protection' resources ignores the reality of existing age inequitability, and further reinforces ageist 'invisibility'. (Decalmer and Glendenning, 1993; Department of Health, 1993)

COUNTER-ARGUMENT

Generic service provision to 'adults at risk' does not preclude the disaggregation of service data for the purpose of monitoring age equitability and taking corrective action. (Slater, 1995)

Obviously, the typology's relative comprehensiveness would have to be gauged by the extent to which the range of different authors' formulations could be reduced to permutations of the essential arguments and counter-arguments presented. However, such a task transcends the main purpose of the present chapter, which is to explore the scope for a synthesised strategy constructed out of differential assessments within each of the four dimensions specified.

A model strategy

At first sight, the typology above might reinforce a 'job lot' mentality of 'elders' versus 'adults' by appearing to imply (or even demand) a straight choice between two mutually exclusive sets of arguments and counter-arguments. But this is an illusion: each dimension of the typology is both logically distinct and methodologically autonomous, opening up the possibility of a differentiated strategy in relation to the elder/adult question. A schematic representation of such a strategy is offered in Figure 1.

Dimension	'Elder' focus	'Adult' focus
I Conceptual specificity	✓	✗
II Legislative priority	✗	✓
III Policy targeting	✓	✓
IV Service equitability	✓	✗

Figure 1 Components of an elder abuse strategy

The horizontal rows of the grid correspond to the four dimensions of the typology detailed above. The vertical columns represent the competing claims of the 'elders' versus 'adults' camps. The cells produced by the intersecting rows and columns constitute discrete options for the synthetic construction of a composite strategy. Ticks and crosses in individual cells convey an immediate visual sense of a composite strategy, albeit rather crudely and in need of detailed elaboration.

Contrary to immediate appearances, the tick/cross configuration in the top row ('conceptual specificity') does not signify that the argument over the analytical versus descriptive status of 'elder abuse' can be conclusively decided in purely intellectual terms. It simply recognises that a campaign concerned with the particular experiences of older people is likely to designate the latter as such – that is, with specific reference to their age status. Explicit arguments to rationalise this designation would then be understood best as intellectual contributions to the task of 'social problem construction' (Blumer, 1971), as opposed to purely 'scientific' accounts of an objective 'discovery'.

By contrast, the reverse cross/tick configuration in the second row ('legislative priority') constitutes an unequivocal stance in favour of an 'adults' focus in statutory reform. This does not suggest a taboo on age reference as such; on the contrary, old age might well be explicitly acknowledged as a particular area of *socially* increased vulnerability, alongside chronic sickness or learning disability, for example. The strategic decision in favour of an over-arching 'adults' focus in law simply implies that individual elders at risk should enjoy the unqualified status of 'adults', as opposed to being constituted as a separate legal subject in their own right.

Given this fundamental proviso on the specifically legislative front, the third row ('policy targeting') can safely be characterised as one of agency choice, as suggested by the dual tick pattern. This would mean that agency and inter-agency deliberations on generic 'adults at risk' and/or specific 'elder abuse' policies would almost inevitably temper intellectual rigour with a strategic eye to the interplay of national policy, local organisational structure and collective user/carer preference.

This said, however, even the generic 'adults' option cannot afford to be 'age blind' in the sense of repressing discussion of generalised age differences. This crucial reservation is given strategic expression via the unequivocal tick/cross configuration in the bottom row of the grid ('service equitability'). In recognition of the reality (albeit far from universal) of age inequality in service delivery, agencies must ensure the generation of age-specific data in respect of referral, assessment and service delivery, so as to be in a position to monitor and promote the effectiveness of any would-be generic policy against known demographic and epidemiological data.

An actual strategy

Drawing together the considerations made above, the strategy implied in Figure 1 aims to transcend the apparent either/or mentality of the 'elders' versus 'adults' debate, and to synthesise a range of divergent, but not inherently antagonistic, arguments into a mutually reinforcing composite. Obviously, interested parties may well take exception to specific components and/or to the specific composite on offer. Hopefully, however, the idea of seeking to arrive at a differentiated judgement in such a complex area as elder abuse will not be repudiated as such. Finally, if readers are inclined to castigate the present author for intellectual arrogance in presuming to undertake such an exercise in the first place, it is important to stress that the following account aims to distil a strategy already emerging, albeit unevenly and unconsciously, within social policy generally and the elder abuse movement in particular.

For example, the 'elder' option indicated in the top row of the grid ('conceptual specificity') correlates with Bennett and Kingston's advocacy of a model unique to elder abuse and neglect, which, as previously noted, has been widely endorsed. Equally influential, to judge by a major study of family violence across the life span (Penhale and Kingston, 1995), is the adoption of Blumer's model of social problem construction, and the explicit attempt to 'legitimate the social problem of elder abuse and neglect' (Bennett and Kingston, 1993, p 10).

Formulated thus, the 'elder' option seems to be global in nature. Indeed, the uniquely later-life model constitutes the 'philosophical basis the authors suggest is used in all circumstances' (Bennett and Kingston, 1993, p 47). From the strategic perspective of the present chapter, however, the relative autonomy of such considerations in the conceptual dimension is confirmed by the fact that the same authors are far from averse to 'adult' initiatives in the dimension designated as 'legislative priority' in the present chapter. On the contrary, Bennett and Kingston implicitly endorse the 'adults' option indicated in the second row of the grid by their positive citation of the Law Commission's emerging proposals for statutory reform in respect of 'vulnerable persons', a development that is discussed at greater length presently.

Moving on to the third row of the grid, the elder/adult equivocation in respect of 'policy targeting' is matched by the relative incidence of 'elder' and 'adult' policies adopted by local authorities: early research revealed an approximately equal split and 'no clear pattern of preference in this respect' (Penhale, 1993, p 14). This picture was confirmed two years later in the results of further research published by Action on Elder Abuse (1995), and not substantially contradicted by a major subsequent update on research from the Age Concern Institute of Gerontology (McCreadie, 1996). This would seem to reflect what one group of authors has termed the 'pragmatic' approach to abuse, where policy decisions are heavily influenced by an agency's existing service base and culture (Biggs et al, 1995, p 19).

In this spirit, local authority representatives attending a Department of Health seminar explicitly endorsed the view that the needs of older people could be addressed equally well via elder or adult policies, depending on existing service structures and priorities. However, a rider was added that 'where a generic adults abuse policy is adopted, a specialist sub-section dealing with abuse of older people would be desirable' (Department of Health, 1995, p 5). This position was simultaneously endorsed by the Association of Directors of Social Services (1995) and reaffirmed at the latter's spring conference two years later (Ambache and Davey, 1997). For its part, Action on Elder Abuse had offered the same advice in its pro forma document for the production of agency policies, procedures and guidelines, which also stressed the need for 'monitoring of both procedures and outcomes' (Action on Elder Abuse, 1995, appendix A).

It is interesting that the accompanying questionnaire sent to health and social services agencies (Action on Elder Abuse, 1995, appendix C) failed to include 'age of victim' in the list of aspects it is particularly interested in monitoring. This is presumably an oversight, as the spirit of the document as a whole – and of the related publications from the Department of Health and the Association of Directors of Social Services – is that elders should be 'visible', particularly when served by generic adult services. While not spelled out as such, this would seem to imply a need for age-specific monitoring of equitability in service provision and take-up, as suggested by the tick/cross configuration in the bottom row of the grid. Needless to say, any such monitoring is crucially dependent on the generation of reliable quantitative data in the first place, the importance of which is underlined in the largest review of elder abuse research to date (McCreadie, 1996, pp 95ff).

The pivotal role of legislative reform

Viewing Figure 1 as a whole, it must be noted that an unequivocal 'adult' stance is recorded in only one row of the grid – 'legislative priority'. The special significance of this dimension requires fuller consideration.

When *The Law and Elderly People* was first published by Age Concern (1986), the prospect of discrete legislation tailored to the specific needs of older people seems to have been assumed as relatively unproblematical. Yet almost ten years later, British legislators had not 'even rehearsed the arguments for and against a bespoke law on elder abuse', and this negative state of affairs was not wholly devoid of rationale: 'it is, to some extent, explainable on the basis that our law has resisted the temptation to categorise older people as a group apart from the rest of society and in need of special attention from the law' (Williams, 1995, p 27).

Meanwhile, the original remit of the Law Commission's work on mental incapacity had been broadened to encompass 'other people who are not incapable of taking their own decisions, but are also especially vulnerable to abuse or neglect from which they are unable to protect themselves' (Law Commission, 1993, p 3). Two years later, the composite report laid before Parliament recommended the following definition:

> A 'vulnerable person' should mean any person of 16 or over who (1) is or may be in need of community care services by reason of mental or other disability, age or illness and who (2) is or may be unable to take care of himself or herself, or unable to protect himself or herself against significant harm or serious exploitation. (Law Commission, 1995, p 159)

By including 'age' as one source of vulnerability, the Law Commission has made a positive response to the representations of the elder abuse campaign. At the same time, however, 'age' is explicitly subsumed under the generic adult auspices of a 'single definition of vulnerability which will apply to all those who should be brought within the scope of the reformed emergency powers'.

Part Nine of the Law Commission report proposes a correspondingly uniform protective framework, based on a duty of social services authorities to investigate and assess informally (in the legal sense of non-recourse to coercive legal powers), but backed up by a step-by-step emergency intervention spectrum of a formal nature. The latter comprises powers of entry and interview, entry warrants, assessment orders, temporary protection orders authorising removal to protective accommodation, and a duty to return the person home as soon as practicable and consistent with their interests.

As already noted, the emerging proposals of the Law Commission have met with near-universal acclaim from elder abuse campaigners. The elder abuse campaign mounted in the trade press actually rejoiced (somewhat prematurely, as it turned out) that 'with the Law Commission blueprint on the table, the bandwagon of legislative change starts to look unstoppable' (Murray, 1993, p 16). More recently, a report on two Department of Health seminars on elder abuse included a paper by the widely published Olive Stevenson, arguing that 'the whole process of intervention should take account of Law Commission principles' (Department of Health, 1995, appendix 1). The radical implications of this exhortation could be taken one step further by the addition of a final phrase in much the same spirit: the whole process of intervention should take account of Law Commission principles in their entirety. In particular, this would ensure explicit acknowledgement of the Law Commission's fundamental principle in respect of the 'objecting client'.

> It is clear that some physically frail and vulnerable people choose, in the exercise of their free will, to refuse services which might (in the view of most people) benefit them. Others choose to remain in situations which appear to others to be causing them unnecessary harm ... Since there is to be a single client group of vulnerable persons, protection for the autonomy of those who do not want help should be expressed as a proviso to the effect that the new powers may not be exercised where the person concerned objects, unless that person is believed to suffer from mental disability. (Law Commission, 1995, p 161)

This spirit is echoed in the subsequent Green Paper on substitute decision making, which emphasises the Government's determination 'to ensure that, if the law in this area is to be reformed, there is an appropriate balance between protecting vulnerable adults and respect for individual rights' (Lord Chancellor's Department, 1997, p v). A welcome side-effect of the generic 'objecting client' principle is that it addresses the reservations voiced by critics of the age-specific focus of the elder abuse campaign. Happily, this is achieved without antagonising the proponents of a model unique to later life at what Bennett and Kingston have termed the 'philosophical' level, and which in the present chapter has been identified as the relatively autonomous dimension of 'conceptual specificity'.

All in all, a radical 'adults' pitch on the specifically legislative front, without prejudice to the need for explicit age specificity in other dimensions (notably 'service equitability'), can be identified as the dominant factor in an overall strategy to promote genuine protection for vulnerable older people, and simultaneously to challenge the oppressive ageist stereotypes that are all too often a contributing factor to that vulnerability. Such a strategy signifies neither victory nor defeat for either 'side' of the adult/elder divide, but the transcendence of global either/or thinking on the subject. The strategy in question is irreducibly hybrid in nature. But then, effective strategies usually are.

Implications for practice

To introduce the theme of 'implications for practice' at this juncture might come as something of a surprise. In the preceding discussion, the dilemmas of the elder/adult divide have been located at the level of national social policy and local agency provision. Whilst the rationale for such a preoccupation with macro considerations has, it is hoped, been established, this might have promoted the misleading impression that the micro level remains unaffected by such considerations. The reality is quite different: whether consciously or unconsciously, direct practice is influenced profoundly by considerations of age. Professional accountability demands that this influence be openly confronted and explicitly justified.

Revisiting the grid in Figure 1, the implications for practice are most readily accessed via what, in row three, has been termed 'policy targeting'. Strategic decisions at this level set the parameters for service response, including a determination as to whether direct intervention is organised under the auspices of 'adults' or 'elders'. Although it is generally conceded that either option can actively promote the interests of older adults at risk of serious harm, when the two different approaches are put into practice they will confront the elder/adult dilemma in quite distinct ways.

The developing critique of ageism (Bytheway, 1995) has uncovered a complex spectrum of structural disadvantage, ranging from straightforward denial of equal resourcing at one extreme to active encroachment on civil liberties at the other. This suggests that workers operating under a generic 'vulnerable adults' policy need to be particularly wary of professional neglect and even denigration of older adults. Oppressive practices of this nature would presumably be unconscious in the vast majority of cases, although American research has identified instances of clinicians explicitly posing the inherently discriminatory question: 'is it worth my time getting involved with a person so old?' (Baumhover and Beall, 1996, p 249). At the other end of the ageist spectrum, workers operating under a specific 'elder abuse' policy might be better advised to guard against the reverse pitfall of paternalistic over-protection, in line with the critique of residential care's tendency to give priority to concern about possible harm over respect for individual freedom in the case of older people (Counsel and Care, 1992).

Meanwhile, striking a happy medium between the two extremes of neglect and interference, agencies that adopt the sort of differentiated strategy advocated in this chapter could well manage the complexities of anti-ageist practice with particular effectiveness via a matrix structure of generic and specialist workers – a model specifically commended in relation to community care provision generally (Smale et al, 1994). Such a matrix would mirror the complex structures within which abuse itself occurs. As research into the implementation of both community care and children's legislation has reminded managers and front-line workers alike, social problems are neither an unmediated expression of individual pathology nor an essential attribute of entire population groups, but the malfunctioning of a network of people. Being old is not a serious problem any more than being a baby is a serious problem, but being either in the absence of appropriate relationships and/or in the presence of positively damaging relationships most certainly is a 'social problem' (Smale et al, 1994, p 73). This perspective is probably most closely associated with social work in its broadest sense.

This emphasis on the social context of 'individual' problems corresponds to what Chris Iveson refers to elsewhere as 'belonging' – that is, the working assumption that individuals belong to a systemic whole made up of its constituent parts and the connections among them. But if older people 'belong', it follows that they must be influencing as well as being influenced by those around them. In other words, if older people are part of a system, they must also share responsibility for whatever is happening in their lives. This second working assumption leads inexorably to a third: if older people share responsibility for the events that make up their lives, they must also be exercising a degree of choice, from which it follows that they must be capable of making other choices.

As Iveson himself openly admits, these working assumptions amount to an act of faith: 'there is no way of knowing that all people retain the capacity to choose, but believing that they do leads to one sort of behaviour and believing that they don't leads to another' (Iveson, 1990, p 16). This holds generally across age boundaries, but is especially precarious in relation to direct work with older adults, which may explain why a book propounding a specific way of working with adults in general is largely illustrated by cases drawn from later life.

It is important to emphasise, however, that the relevance of age to direct practice with older adults is not simply a matter of combating ageism; competent practice is simultaneously based on the positive principle of 'working with difference'. From this perspective, people's 'race', gender and other shared characteristics are not simply a battleground for social power struggles in general, but also constitute the complex building blocks of individual identity. With reference to working with age difference, direct practice involves actively reinforcing the personal resources built up and periodically reconstituted over a lifetime that will invariably exceed that of the worker by several years or even decades. Respecting and promoting older people's sense of themselves as dynamic participants in their home life and wider social networks crucially depends on the explicit location of each person within this 'life history' (Hughes, 1995, p 28).

Suspicion or discovery of abuse obviously has dramatic relevance to professional assessment and intervention, but must not be allowed to negate the general principles of anti-ageist practice. In relation to vulnerable adults generally, the Law Commission has stressed the need to actively promote a person's ability to participate fully in any decisions affecting them. With particular relevance to the vexed issue of dementia, this entails due regard to 'the ascertainable past and present wishes and feelings of the person concerned, and the factors that person would consider if able to do so' (Law Commission, 1995, p 44). This recommendation simultaneously repudiates the oppressive assumption of global incapacity and actively reinforces the dynamic significance of 'life history'.

As noted earlier, Olive Stevenson has been particularly active in advocating the incorporation of Law Commission principles into all aspects of elder abuse work. Additionally, as quoted at the outset of this chapter, she has encouraged readers to confront the dilemmas inherent in singling out older adults for special consideration. In an important contribution to a volume on developing services for older people and their families, she has attempted to steer a careful course between the Scylla of romantically denying the 'compressed morbidity' of old age and the Charybdis of oppressively assuming global decrepitude. Older people need to be viewed as 'both the same and different' (Stevenson, 1996, p 208). Happily, this dual perspective coincides with the differentiated elder/adult strategy at the heart of the present chapter and represented diagrammatically in Figure 1.

Conclusion

Olive Stevenson's healthy reminder of the complexities of genuinely anti-ageist practice with older people echoes the tenor of a pioneering study on the law and vulnerable elderly people from the mid-1980s. On this occasion, Sally Greengross' preface offered a personal litmus test for evaluating proposals made in the name of older people, a group to which most readers are ultimately destined to be assigned:

> In seeking to give them a stronger voice this report raises a number of questions and highlights certain dilemmas we all must face if we are to ensure to vulnerable old people a quality of life we would find acceptable ourselves. One day any one of us may be amongst those people forced to experience our success or failure in achieving this. (Age Concern England, 1986, p 6)

Readers of the present chapter are invited to consider its arguments in the same light – as potential users of a protective framework on offer. In the capacity of 'adults', readers have a right to form autonomous judgements. The residual question is: to what extent would they wish to curtail that right in anticipation of their own old age?

Tackling elder abuse together: developing joint policies and procedures

Christabel Shawcross

There has been little central government policy advice and guidance concerning elder abuse. Local authorities have taken a lead in encouraging other key agencies to develop joint policies and procedures. Research has been minimal, in stark contrast to child abuse, despite the fact that abuse of older people occurs in people's own homes and group care settings. Responsibility for preventing and responding to abuse has to be a national and local concern on a multi-agency basis. This must include key statutory social service and health agencies as well as independent providers of care. Because of the multifarious nature of abuse, a wide range of agencies – including the police, legal advisers, Social Security and advocacy organisations – must be involved. This chapter examines national and local developments, considers the research and points to ways forward.

Background to developments

In 1984, when concern about elder abuse in the UK was raised with the publication of *Old Age Abuse* (Eastman, 1984), it reflected views of social services staff by highlighting the potential abuse that older people could face in their own homes. However, this growing professional concern met with little response from central government. This contrasted with government reaction (through the Department of Health) to child abuse: this subject has had a high profile, with clear national guidelines and policy framework backed by new legislation that was a feature of the 1980s. The attention given to the protection of children is, of course, essential but contrasted starkly with that given to older people. This difference may best be explained by differing priorities that are partly a function of ageism and ageist attitudes. However, there was progress in residential care with the Registered Homes Act 1984 and the accompanying code of practice *Home Life* (Centre for Policy on Ageing, 1984). As a first measure the Registered Homes Act was of great significance, but it was more to do with setting minimum standards in the independent sector and had no force in homes run by local authorities; moreover, *Home Life* made no mention of abuse.

The initiative to move the agenda forward came from various agencies, both voluntary and professional, publicising their common concerns. The legislation was a fundamental concern and resulted in the Age Concern England publication *The Law and Vulnerable People* (1986). A joint working party set up by the British Geriatrics Society in the early 1990s was the first attempt at a national multi-agency approach to address elder abuse, and included the Carers National Association. The working party collaborated on the production of guidelines for multi-agency action and a leaflet for carers. In 1991 the Association of Directors of Social Services published their guidelines *Adults At Risk*. Also in 1991, the Department of Health commissioned a research review, *Elder Abuse: An exploratory study* (McCreadie, 1991). This last was important in demonstrating how confused the issue was, with no agreed definitions of abuse, and highlighting that little research had been carried out in the UK compared with the USA which already had well-established adult protection legislation. The first response from the Social Services Inspectorate, an arm of the Department of Health, was a study of how two local authorities were addressing the issues of elder abuse in domestic settings (Social Services Inspectorate, 1992). Not surprisingly, this found that there was a lack of policy and guidance on intervention. Whilst the Department of Health, through the Social Services Inspectorate, continued to issue advice and guidelines on standards for residential care homes (Social Services Inspectorate, 1989), there was still nothing specific on how to prevent and recognise abuse in residential care.

Current community care policy, under the terms of the National Health Service and Community Care Act 1990, has resulted in the independent sector becoming major providers of state-funded care in both residential and domestic settings. It has also had an impact on concerns about the abuse of older people. A positive requirement of the new policy was that residential homes run by local authorities had to be inspected although they were not forced to be registered. Undoubtedly the outstanding gap in community care policy, in terms of missed opportunities to offer protection to the most vulnerable consumers of social care services, was the refusal of central government to require the registration and inspection of home care agencies. Such a requirement might not have sat easily with a government determined on a policy of deregulation, but many agencies were convinced that, in this area at least, further regulation was justified.

The legislative framework

The legislation that provides the framework for agencies to work together to tackle elder abuse does not really facilitate implementing joint action. It is diverse, fragmented and diffuse, because there is no single piece of legislation that relates to protecting older people. Moreover, abuse itself has no nationally agreed definition and can take many forms, from physical to financial. It is essential for agencies to agree together how to interpret and use the legislation in practice. Responses will vary according to where the abuse occurs and the characteristics of the victim as well as the type of abuse perpetrated. The use of legislation, however, must be within a framework of values that have as an overriding principle that older people are people first, who are citizens who have rights that must be respected. The fundamental dilemma and challenge is where competence and the capacity to understand and consent have to be judged. Detailed agreement must be reached on circumstances that warrant invoking formal competency procedures through the Court of Protection. Equally important are agreements with local police and legal representatives on how to use evidence from mentally frail older people whose competence could be disputed in court proceedings.

The legal framework for regulating residential and nursing home care, bolstered by guidance and standards for care, is clearer. What is less clear is how abuse in such settings can be uncovered. Local guidelines need to determine the respective roles of the registration unit, the home and the social services department. In settings where 24-hour care is provided, the inspection of registered homes can provide some protection, but abuse can be hidden, insidious and colluded on by staff. It is usually external visitors such as relatives or friends who reveal instances of abuse. The recent exposure of extensive networks of abusers in children's homes shows that there is no room for complacency; indeed the lesson must be how to ensure that there is no cause for similar scandals to emerge in older people's homes. There is also an important gap in protection where hospital settings do not have a regulatory system to maintain basic standards; the Patients' Charter is a start but is not subject to external scrutiny.

The campaign by Age Concern England for a change in the law culminated in the Law Commission report (1995) that proposed increasing the powers of local authorities to intervene to protect vulnerable people. A response from government as to whether to take forward its proposals has been long awaited, and at the time of writing a Green Paper is due. If these proposals are enacted, there will have to be national policy guidelines on multi-agency work because local authorities would need to act jointly with other welfare agencies, which might need to be required to do so by law. Increasing the powers of local authorities is likely to raise issues about state intervention similar to those in child protection and will require national debate. Questions such as who defines whether abuse has occurred, how to gain entry, who decides to override users' and/or carers' views need to be answered. The danger is that attention will focus unduly on procedural rectitude at the expense of tangible outcomes. Social workers are sometimes told of concerns by a victim but asked not do anything because the importance of the relationship with the alleged abuser outweighs the pain of the abuse in the victim's eyes. Some abuse may have a long history, such as with domestic violence. These are all, of course, relevant issues now, and more difficult to tackle in the absence of a national policy but essential to discuss in the formulation of local policies. Nevertheless, a key lesson comes from the North American experience of adult protection policies where over-emphasis on procedures and reporting takes up considerable resources and leaves less time for negotiating satisfactory solutions.

Researching the subject

Research into the incidence and prevalence of elder abuse has been undertaken only relatively recently; an excellent review of existing literature is given by *Elder Abuse: Update on research* (McCreadie, 1996). It draws together a wide range of material and makes a coherent and succinct analysis of the dilemmas facing policy makers and practitioners. McCreadie highlights the key difficulty for agencies developing joint guidelines in reaching agreement on definitions by quoting several different ways of describing what is meant by abuse. She states 'under the umbrella of "abuse" there is a diversity of complex experience' (p 1). The fundamental problem is, as has already been highlighted, that there is no legal definition. Whilst agreements can be reached by agencies on their own definitions, responses will be restricted because of the limited legal powers.

There is a useful chapter on abuse in communal settings, which looks at what can be learned from research into factors contributing to abuse in residential and other settings. McCreadie demonstrates the difficulty there is again with definitions and how aspects of abuse and standards of care are interwoven. Multi-agency working must clearly involve registration and inspection units, which have a crucial role to play in investigating allegations of abuse in residential and nursing home care. Inspection units operated jointly by local and health authorities provide an advantage in enabling abuse to be tackled together. However, the Social Service Inspectorate's own inspections have revealed that there is wide variation in resources allocated to inspection units; few were able to carry out their required number of visits. Clearly it cannot be assumed that they will always be able to identify abuse as part of their routine work, particularly where it may be covert and hidden.

In domestic settings, research has contributed to a better understanding of risk factors, with a clear move away from carer stress to looking at the history of family relationships and the characteristics of the abuser rather than those of the victim. The presence of a relative with a drug, alcohol or mental health problem may be a more important indicator than a frail older person with dementia. What is needed from research is a greater understanding of the interaction of these factors as well as an evaluation of the results of interventions to inform multi-agency work.

Recent national and policy developments

Over the past few years there has been slow but continuing progress in response to the growing awareness of elder abuse. The national lead by the Department of Health is best described as a cautious approach at a time when efforts were concentrating on the implementation of the community care reforms. The publication of the Social Services Inspectorate national practice guidelines *No Longer Afraid* (1993a), based on extensive consultation on a multi-agency basis, was an important milestone. However, these are practice guidelines that provide a framework in which local authorities can develop their own guidelines rather than, as in child protection, mandatory guidance agreed nationally. A significant omission, which has not been addressed, is a framework for a coherent approach to abuse in residential settings.

The guidelines (Social Services Inspectorate, 1993a) were important in distilling best practice from procedures already in use, and undoubtedly acted as a catalyst to social services departments that were only beginning to address the issue. A key point was the emphasis on dealing with abuse in the context of community care assessments and service provision. It is rightly cautious about the need to go down the prescriptive and procedural route of child protection. Apart from obvious reasons that protecting adults cannot be seen in the same way as protecting children, there would be significant resource implications in setting up cumbersome and time-consuming procedures.

Concern over the need for social services departments to recognise abuse was reflected in other Social Service Inspectorate documents: in residential care for older people (1993c), and in quality standards for home support – 'Home support workers will need to be familiar with the indicators of abuse' (1993b, p 23). Counsel and Care (1994) also highlighted a range of issues in a series of discussion papers.

A continuing role in raising awareness of abuse was taken by Age Concern England with the setting up, in 1993, of Action on Elder Abuse, which also received funding from the Department of Health. Action on Elder Abuse has campaigned to raise awareness of the issues, developed a network of committed agencies and individuals, and promoted the development of guidelines through the report of a survey, *Everybody's Business* (Action on Elder Abuse, 1995). The most recent development – the piloting and subsequent national launch of Action on Elder Abuse's helpline – is likely to be a catalyst for local agencies to review their responses to allegations of abuse.

A key multi-agency initiative by Action on Elder Abuse is their pamphlet (1996) on abuse; it is for all workers in the community to raise awareness and to encourage providers to have policies. A similar pamphlet is in preparation for workers in communal settings.

Unlike other areas of abuse, there is no campaign by service users to raise the profile of concerns from older people themselves. It is encouraging that an analysis of the helpline, *Hearing the Despair* (Family Policy Studies Centre, 1997), showed that 16.5 per cent of the 550 calls received were from older victims. Workers in the four pilot sites concluded that the helpline 'had not increased demands made on their organisation as a whole, although co-ordination and planning at a strategic level had increased' (p 4).

What is known about joint policies and procedures?

The overview of research by Action on Elder Abuse (1995) describes how several previous surveys (eg Penhale, 1993) had revealed that, although most social services departments were developing guidelines, many were only in draft form. Of particular concern was the continuing lack of awareness shown by health authorities and trusts. Whilst the Action on Elder Abuse survey had an improved response rate, several health agencies did not think there was any need for themselves to develop operational policies. In addition, 'the impression given by the majority of respondents was [that] this is a provider issue' (Action on Elder Abuse, 1995, p 13). This seems to imply an abrogation of purchasing responsibility to be clear about standards and responsibilities. However, it may partly reflect the fact that there has been no central advice or guidance to health authorities to raise awareness. Action on Elder Abuse made several recommendations, including the 'commitment of all agencies involved to multi-agency and inter-agency collaboration' (p 23).

In the absence of law reform or further guidance from the Department of Health, the Association of Directors of Social Services published a discussion document, *Mistreatment of Older People* (1995), to stimulate debate on how to take the issue forward. It usefully puts the issue of dealing with abuse into the context of the changing nature of social care provision from monopolistic providers to the proliferation of agencies as part of the contract culture. The Association is concerned to ensure that the development of regulatory and contractual systems are in concord. It notes that 'a balance has to be struck in avoiding overly prescriptive and bureaucratic systems imposed upon providers whilst protecting vulnerable users and preventing mistreatment' (p 12).

More recently, the Association of Directors of Social Services' spring conference in 1997 passed a resolution on responding to the abuse of vulnerable adults. It stated that the Association would take a lead in developing a coherent and comprehensive national policy and that the response to abuse should be of an inter-agency nature. The Association will pursue the work with other key national bodies, including the Department of Health. The intention is to encourage a stronger lead from central government, including an emphasis on other key agencies, particularly the police and the NHS.

With whom should policies be developed?

This is a key question: it will need to be answered locally to reflect local circumstances but must embrace commissioners, purchasers and providers of health and social care. Other agencies may include the police, housing and benefits agencies, depending on the nature of the abuse. Policies concerning domestic violence will also have to be taken into account. Whilst *No Longer Afraid* addressed this, there were no similar guidelines issued to other key agencies. The development of health agencies into separate trusts covering hospitals and community health services as well as GP fundholders means it is a complicated process. The range of agencies involved will also reflect how ambitious and inclusive policies aim to be. If a comprehensive approach is taken to raise awareness generally – and it is argued that this should be the case – a clear strategy must be formulated that addresses not just the drawing up of procedures to respond to allegations of abuse but also how to prevent it from happening and engaging in local initiatives to gain public support.

Social services departments with a corporate approach within their local authority (ie co-ordinating action across all departments) are in a good position to provide a lead, but it should not be seen as solely their responsibility. Tackling how to prevent abuse can be done only on a collaborative basis through close partnership with local agencies. Local authorities are developing corporate ways of promoting safer environments and, using this objective, social services departments could highlight ways of preventing abuse of older people. Moreover, social services need to work with housing departments and associations to ensure that all staff in contact with older people are aware of the issues. Wider community concerns such as combating racial abuse, vandalism and youth gang harassment are also seen as relevant to broad definitions of elder abuse (Pritchard, 1995). Strategies to deal with these problems will have to engage with local education services, youth workers and community police officers. An important feature is to raise awareness by using the local media to publicise and promote local initiatives.

The involvement and commitment of local voluntary organisations representing both users and carers are crucial to the success of developing policies and procedures that recognise people's needs and deploy services accordingly.

What should policies and procedures address?

For the purpose of inter-agency co-operation it is important that agreements on philosophy and values are fundamental to the formulation of policy. This, whilst separate from procedural matters, provides the framework to underpin joint guidelines. These guidelines need to be based on values promoting the rights of older people, however vulnerable, and reflect the fact that older people are not a homogenous group but are as heterogeneous as the rest of the population in a multi-cultural society. Equal opportunity principles ensuring that race, culture and gender issues inform policies are essential. Increasingly, older people with learning disabilities, mental health problems or dementia have particular needs to consider. This is especially important in terms of how to ensure a balancing of objectives such as protection and empowerment. It is not the intention here to propose model frameworks, as there are now many examples and *No Longer Afraid* provides a sound basis. Whilst there is no point in reinventing the wheel, there are invaluable benefits in agencies jointly discussing their understanding of indicators, definitions and legislation to agree on responses.

A fundamental purpose of joint procedures is to ensure that front-line staff have a clear framework that facilitates and supports their professional judgements on what action to take to protect victims. Responses to allegations of abuse in domestic settings need to clarify the interface between an investigation, a community care assessment of need and, in cases of mental illness, the care programme approach. Balancing prevention, protection and punishment can be precarious. Agreeing definitions of abuse and how these are determined needs to be a continual process, and learning from local experience will be crucial in the absence of ongoing national research. These areas were all highlighted in an abuse seminar report from the Social Services Inspectorate, which provides an action checklist for cross-agency working. It emphasises that 'Effective strategies for preventing and responding to abuse of older people requires co-ordinated attention from a wide range of agencies and disciplines'. This should ensure that 'Common ground is identified, a spirit of trust engendered, and the experience of and restrictions on each authority and agency are acknowledged, shared and built on' (Social Services Inspectorate, 1995, p 16).

An important area requiring further work concerns financial abuse, a form of abuse particularly difficult to confront and prove except in the most obvious of cases. Research for the Anchor Housing Trust (Langan and Means, 1994) into personal finances and elderly people with dementia found a complex variety of arrangements. The report concluded that local authorities should review their arrangements on receivership and appointeeship, 'including how consistent these are with emerging policies on elder abuse' (p 27). These also need to be consistent with local policies on managing people's money and take into account how they are reflected in purchasing contracts with all types of providers. Local agencies that may be involved can range from the Benefits Agency and post offices to banks.

Agreeing joint procedures for responses to abuse in residential and other care settings is equally complicated. The Action on Elder Abuse survey (1994, p 16) found 'Only one in five documents received from all sources covered abuse in all these settings'. Although care homes in the independent sector are subject to registration and inspection and local authority homes to inspection, this is not an effective measure, on its own, for highlighting poor quality care. There must be local agreement, involving social services and health registration units, local authority advisory panels and representatives of providers. The fundamental concern is to ensure that the victim is protected immediately and that adequate representation of their views is arranged. Abuse in care settings can be the result of institutional regimes with poor standards and inadequate training, or concerted actions by individuals to intimidate or harass. Procedures must determine what triggers the implementation of abuse guidelines, who will be involved in investigations and what action should be taken if abuse is confirmed. This is highly complex, and potentially confusing, terrain. Consideration has to be given to the interface between organisations' complaints and disciplinary procedures and external abuse procedures, in order to ensure that one does not prejudice the other. Although complaints must be reported to registration units, the degree of their involvement will vary, and confidentiality limits how far information can be shared. This is a particular issue for people who are placed in homes outside their area, where purchasers may not be informed of concerns.

What lessons can be learned from child protection?

All local authorities have a long experience of developing child protection guidelines on a multi-agency basis but there is little in the literature to provide a framework for considering the lessons to be learned. It is salutary to note that the current debate on child protection is on how to shift to preventive family services rather than concentrating on protection. This may well prove to be a major lesson. Professional opinion is divided, however, as demonstrated in the Social Services Inspectorate seminar report (1995). It would seem that there is a danger of social services departments, divided into separate adults' and children's divisions, not learning from the full range of experiences associated with decades of child protection procedures. Stevenson's examination of these experiences shows that 'proceduralisation' of child protection has been the main development over 20 years; whilst systems may have protected children, there is a heavy sense of organisational 'burden' (Stevenson, 1996a, p 5).

The obvious difference from elder abuse is the clear legal and policy framework underpinning procedures. Stevenson (1996a) highlights this key area of difference between protecting children and older people in her analysis of the risk, as opposed to the welfare model of protection. She discusses other significant differences such as rights and responsibilities where adults, unlike children, are deemed to be competent unless it is legally shown to be otherwise. In contrast, the responsibility of parents is well defined legally whereas it is not for adults as carers. There are also moral dilemmas concerning the definition of a carer and whether they took on the responsibilities willingly or reluctantly, and whether sufficient support was available. Another problem is that, in contrast to child care, there is no common understanding of 'good-enough caring'.

In Stevenson's view 'the dominance of the risk model in child protection has resulted in responses that are anxiety driven ... The public reaction to child abuse cases and to professionals has powerfully accentuated these responses' (1996a, p 7). In taking a further look at advantages and disadvantages, she clearly favours the welfare approach when addressing the abuse of older people, on the basis that 'it is more likely to contribute to the protection of elders than a single minded concentration upon "risk" even though elements of risk assessment may be required' (p 18).

Whilst there are many dissimilarities between child abuse and abuse of older people, the obvious similarity is in the area of inter-agency work that provides a model on which social services departments can base and monitor their work. Most will undoubtedly wish to develop processes that are flexible enough to deal with the wide variety of situations that will occur, while ensuring that staff have clear and supportive procedures in which to operate. Multi-agency co-operation is a continuous, and at times fraught, process, particularly when differing priorities emerge. In a summary of her report to a conference, Stevenson identifies one of the main similarities as co-operation. 'First, effective co-operative activity will not be effected without an element of proceduralisation, and inter-agency training. The involvement of key professional groups is crucial and not always easy to achieve' (Stevenson, 1996b, p 12). Case conferences as a mechanism will need to be developed. A particularly difficult issue for social services departments, already struggling to service the large number of older people with care packages, concerns the way in which abuse in particular is acknowledged and addressed, often in the face of denial and resistance from the victim.

If values such as empowerment are to be reflected in procedures, close consideration has to be given to the user's involvement in the processes, particularly case conferences. Stevenson discusses the obvious difficulties of how someone who is frail, possibly with seeing or hearing difficulties, can participate meaningfully. She suggests that individual advocates might be appropriate, although advocacy schemes tend to have focused more on younger people and is an area in need of expanding, especially where an older person has dementia.

A less clear area relates to carer involvement. Parents are seen as clearly having rights to attend conferences because of the legal nature of their responsibilities. With older people, responsibilities, and therefore rights, of carers are not legally defined with such clarity. Nevertheless, there is a need to start, as far as possible, on the basis of a partnership with carers as the underpinning principle, which will then need to be reviewed depending on the nature of the relationship and type of abuse identified. Carers, who are often older women, can be victims too.

What about the outcomes?

The process of agencies agreeing what they are doing, and why, is important in order to establish a clear understanding of what is meant by tackling abuse together locally. However, this, in a sense, is just the beginning. Most social services departments have some type of procedure but there is little research into their relative effectiveness. There is even less research into the outcomes for older people who are subjected to abuse. The first detailed research into procedures, with further work forthcoming, comes from the study *Implementing Adult Protection Policies in Kent and East Sussex* (Brown and Stein, 1997). Although the focus was the development of adult protection procedures generally, the findings are also of relevance to the procedures aimed at older people in particular, as consideration was given to a range of distinct client groups. Abuse in domestic and in communal settings were examined separately. Interesting messages emerged from the comparison between the two social services departments on reporting and responding. Kent, although larger, reported significantly fewer cases than East Sussex, and there was no obvious explanation for this. However, the reverse was the case for numbers of referrals going through to case conferences. This clearly underlines the importance of agencies agreeing on what should be reported as suspected abuse, although it is equally important to achieve a balance between that and allowing flexibility of response that also offers adequate protection. A clear framework is required in which professionals can make judgements, involving the victim and their advocate, to achieve an outcome that reflects their wishes. The end-result may be acceptance of the risk, because the victim might fear losing independence by going into a residential setting. However, far too little is known about the success or otherwise about interventions; inter-agency guidelines should, at the least, have sections on how to monitor and review the outcomes of local strategies.

A fundamental objective of inter-agency guidelines must be to ensure that effective communication between agencies is achieved, at both strategic and individual case levels. This may be the key lesson to learn from the failures in the child protection system: enquiry after enquiry has found communication between key agencies and professionals to be inadequate, despite the clear guidance in *Working Together* (Department of Health, 1991). The benefits of such collaboration are tangible: research has established that, where appropriate systems of communication are in place, there is 'a high degree of consensus amongst the professionals about the decisions taken' (Stevenson, 1996a, p 10).

Brown and Stein also discuss the tension that exists between a bureaucratic as opposed to a tea-and-sympathy approach. They conclude 'Flexibility to move between informal and formal approaches ... is the key to consistent reporting' (Brown and Stein, 1997, p 18). Looking at the implications for workload and resource planning, they found that budgets needed to be flexible – not just to meet predicted needs for community care services but also to provide innovative and rapid responses to vulnerable people who had been abused. This continues to be a challenge for budget holders. In emphasising the value of continued monitoring of procedures they state that 'continued monitoring ... will help these counties to develop practice and management of adult protection cases and also to establish norms which might be used for comparison by other authorities' (p 22).

As is known from child protection, standing inter-agency committees have a valuable role in co-ordinating and identifying areas of difficulty. Whilst there is a much clearer framework to work within, partly because of child protection registers, similar structures could be developed for elder abuse cases, although the idea of elder abuse registers is problematic and debatable in the absence of a legal framework. In an article in *Community Care*, it was reported that those involved in the Kent research believe that a 'standing inter-agency group should be set up ... to keep a watching brief and monitor the extent and outcomes of adult protection cases' (Brown et al, 1996, pp 28–29).

Looking to the twenty-first century

It is not known whether there will be legislative changes in the future, although at the time of writing a Green Paper is awaited. If laws are passed, they can take several years to implement, so it is imperative that all agencies build on and develop their inter-agency approaches to be well placed for influencing any legislative and policy changes. National bodies such as the Department of Health, Social Services Inspectorate and the Association of Directors of Social Services must continue to examine and evaluate what is already happening so that best practice can determine and shape future developments. Caution is also required lest legislative changes be seen as a panacea; such solutions often bring different problems.

It is worth noting that, while the RSPCA has clear legal powers (based on nineteenth century legislation) in respect of the protection of animals from abuse, it is currently involved in a fierce debate on the balance of resources between animal welfare and prosecutions (Wallis, 1997, pp 24–32).

Whilst legal changes imposing a duty and power on a local authority to investigate may be essential to protect the most vulnerable, it would be to no one's benefit if a rigid and constricting system were to emerge. The demographic figures for the older population show that, over the next 20 years, there will be a growth in the number of older people from minority ethnic communities and in those who are aged over 85. Research into the incidence and prevalence of abuse should be given priority by the Department of Health to inform future developments at national policy level. Research into the effectiveness of different interventions is needed to assist in the best distribution of resources to tackle elder abuse. The current prospect for social services departments, with reducing resources targeted on those most in need, is of a smaller number of people receiving a higher level of service. This makes it even more important to develop preventive strategies as well as incorporating a welfare approach rather than one that is procedural and based purely on risk management.

Crucially, agencies need to decide how their resources can be used together to combat abuse. In domestic settings, a major commitment by government to combating abuse would be to require the registration and inspection of home care providers. Social services departments with flexible services to support carers and improved care management, with review and monitoring mechanisms involving all providers, can increase the opportunities to identify and support people at risk. The joint training of staff from all agencies is essential to achieve a consistent approach.

In group settings – both residential and day centre based – the training of staff to improve standards of care and to recognise when practices might be abusive should be a high priority. This training must be accompanied by effective systems that encourage and enable people to speak out, particularly the older person affected or their relative. Locally agreed systems for 'whistle-blowing' are important for raising confidence among staff, who, along with the victim and the relative, are often fearful of recriminations for doing so.

There is no room for complacency, because multi-agency guidelines are still not well developed. This was highlighted, significantly, in the annual report from the Social Services Inspectorate Chief Inspector, *Better Management, Better Care*: 'Social services agencies vary widely in their progress in this area' (Department of Health, 1997). Quoting American research into elder abuse projects, McCreadie concluded, 'Inter agency co-ordination is critical to the success of a project. No single agency has all the resources to resolve difficult cases of elder abuse. Therefore co-operation between agencies is the most critical contributor to the success or failure of a project' (McCreadie, 1991, p 50). Whatever the future brings with regard to legislative or policy changes, successful implementation will depend on multi-agency part-nerships taking joint responsibility to tackle elder abuse together. The Department of Health will need to provide clear guidance to ensure that all agencies give this priority. Social services departments, there-fore, have a key responsibility to show the way forward into the twenty-first century.

Author's note

The views expressed in this chapter are personal, and not necessarily those of the London Borough of Barnet.

chapter 5

Elder abuse and participation: a crucial coupling for change

Suzy Croft and Peter Beresford

Abuse has played a central role in the shaping of post-war personal social services and social care. Scandals and inquiries have been a defining feature of their history. Abuse has been routine rather than exceptional. A review of the pages of *Community Care* magazine since its inception over 25 years ago shows abuse featuring on a regular weekly basis, older people being a key target.

The starting point for discussion about elder abuse is an intensely personal experience that is likely to be shocking, distressing, demeaning and painful for those who suffer it. It is important that such discussion is always firmly rooted in this experience, includes it as far as possible in its own process and working, and explores the links between it and broader social, political, structural and human issues. For this reason we begin with a personal experience that has helped to form our focus on elder abuse and *participation*.

Cousin Eve

With the onset of Alzheimer's disease, our cousin Eve, now in her early 80s, had been moved from the sheltered accommodation she lived in, run by a large national charity, to a residential home which it also provided. We had begun to worry about her. She said she was afraid that she would have to move – they had told her twice that she would have to. She was upset that she no longer had her corset, and replacements we had brought were never to be found. The home also discouraged residents from wearing tights, preferring elasticated stockings. To keep her stockings up, Eve had tied them at the top with bits of cloth. Her false teeth had been lost; she had been due to go to the dentist the previous week but when one of us (Suzy Croft) went to see her, she hadn't been.

I decided to check with the head of home about a dental appointment a member of staff had mentioned for the following Monday. The head of home wouldn't stop to talk, so I asked her, as she went backwards and forwards between the dining room and TV room, getting some rice pudding: 'Excuse me, is Eve having her teeth fitted when she goes to the dentist?' 'I don't know', she said. 'I don't know anything about it. I don't go to the dentist. I'm not the dentist. I'm the matron. It's nothing to do with me.' I said, 'Could you just confirm to me that this trip she will have her teeth fitted?' The reply was, 'I've no idea and I'm not negotiating with you.'

Then she walked back across the hall, still talking. I caught up with her and said, 'I'm sorry, I just can't hear what you are saying.' She shouted: 'Do you want to force the words out of my throat? Who do you think you are?' I said, 'All I want is a civil answer to my questions.' She grabbed hold of my wrists. 'I'm going to get you out of here.' She pushed me into the ladies' lavatory, which didn't have a door. I struggled to get away. In the struggle she cut my lip. At one point I was very conscious that she was pulling my hair very hard and I suddenly realised that she was trying to grab the bottom of my left leg. It all took place in a matter of seconds. Two women care assistants said. 'Oh, stop it. Oh, come on now. Oh, stop it', and one tried to pull her hand off my wrist. They tried to get hold of her. I was very frightened because I thought she was going to trip me over or kick me in the stomach. I pulled myself off and said 'I shall report this', and walked back into the visitors' room. When I went in, one of the visitors there said, 'You've cut your lip, dear. Did you realise it's bleeding?' One of the two workers who had tried to get the head of home off me unlocked the entrance to let me out.

The particular circumstances of this incident were that I was heavily pregnant; my daughter was expected and born ten days later. The home was run by a highly respected voluntary organisation. There were witnesses to what happened. The police were called, statements were taken, a medical report provided and inquiries were made, but no charges were brought. As far as we know, no disciplinary action was taken against the head of home, although some time later she was replaced. I was told that I should have complained sooner, but the birth of our baby and my subsequent illness prevented it.

However, these events also raise much broader issues. First, fundamental problems emerge in securing effective redress in settings where the rights and needs of people identified as particularly vulnerable should be safeguarded. Second, issues of gender can be seen to be central. All the actors on this occasion were women, reflecting wider structures of formal 'care', the sexual division of 'informal caring' and the make-up of the elderly population. Finally, if this incident could happen in public, in daytime, to an outside visitor, what does it say about the security and well-being of the residents of such a home? Issues of power and inequalities of power clearly need to be kept centre stage in any discussion of elder abuse. We will argue that these relate to three key components for preventing and challenging elder abuse: the *voice, choice* and *credibility* of older people. (We return to these later.) Our discussion develops the argument that the most effective way to challenge elder abuse, in relation both to individual older people and to older people as a constituency, is by enhancing their say and involvement, both in social care, welfare and public policy specifically and in society more generally. Such participation offers older people, like other groups who experience abuse (notably children, young people and people with learning difficulties), the most effective way of protecting their rights and of keeping control over their lives.

Conceptualising elder abuse

We don't intend to add to the general debate about the definition and conceptualisation of elder abuse, which is available elsewhere in this book and more generally. Elder abuse tends to be categorised in terms of physical, psychological, sexual and material/financial abuse and active and passive neglect (Biggs et al, 1995, pp 36–37; McCreadie, 1996a, pp 9–19). Distinctions are also drawn between elder abuse in domestic and in institutional and formal care settings. However, there is one general point that we should make relating to the latter, because it informs our discussion. We see all elder abuse – both domestic and institutional – as relating to public policy and provision. Ultimately this determines the likelihood of abuse in both domestic and institutional settings. Each is linked to the nature, quality and adequacy of policy and provision to support older people, both as they relate to older people themselves, as potential subjects of abuse, and to those who may abuse or neglect them, for want of adequate and appropriate services and support. Such an approach to elder abuse prioritises responses based on specific public policy measures to prevent and ameliorate it as well as on broader changes in social and cultural values and priorities.

The professional discussion of elder abuse

So far, most attention has been focused on professional and organisational measures to counter elder abuse. Training for practitioners has been seen as a key way of both preventing and challenging elder abuse (eg Pritchard, 1992; Baumhover and Beall, 1996). This follows a similar approach in the context of child abuse, which so far has shown little sign of success. Significantly, as is often the case in welfare, the proposals made have been largely of social administrative change (eg Schlesinger and Schlesinger, 1988; McCreadie, 1996a). The main response has been a 'technicist' one, as reflected in proposals for:

- screening and regular assessment by health and other professionals;
- the identification of research as 'the key to preventive strategies' (Bennett and Kingston, 1993);

- improved discharge planning and 'prognosis' assessment (Baumhover and Beall, 1996);
- more conventional social care services such as day, respite and short-term care and domiciliary services, as well as appropriate procedures, support from agency and managers, case planning, monitoring and review, inter-professional liaison and collaboration (Pritchard, 1992; McCreadie, 1996b);
- model projects for dealing with elder abuse and mandatory reporting of elder abuse when it is identified (Wolf and Pillemer, 1989).

Connecting elder abuse and participation

So far, debates about and policy developments for elder abuse and participation have largely been separate from and unrelated to each other. There has been some recognition of the importance of participation in this context – for example, Phil Slater has highlighted the need for 'user involvement' to challenge 'power imbalances institutionalised in existing "elderly" services' (Slater, 1992), and there has been some rhetorical commitment to involvement in official statements – but participation has not generally been identified as a central issue in understanding, preventing or addressing elder abuse. Little detailed attention has been paid so far to participation in discussions about elder abuse. Similarly, although there has been some discussion of the importance of 'empowering' elders to address the problem, this has often shared a more general failing of neither clarifying the term nor offering agreed and effective strategies for achieving it. It is important to take forward the process of connecting the discourses of elder abuse and participation, and this is our main concern here. A primary requirement for doing this is to examine closely the concept and practice of participation. As yet this does not seem to have been done in the context of elder abuse.

Participation: two competing approaches

Whilst participation has gained increasing importance in a wide range of political, policy and theoretical debates, both its analysis and its implementation have been hesitant and limited. There is still little agreement about the meaning or purpose of 'participation' and it continues to be dogged by much ambiguity and distrust. There has also been a frequent failure to connect discourses on participation in different disciplines and areas of activity (Croft and Beresford, 1992). Some of the most significant progress on participation, however, has been made in the field of social care and social services. Ideas of 'user involvement', 'user-centred' and 'user-led' policy and services have achieved particular prominence in professional and political debates about social and community care. Provisions for comment and consultation have been built into legislation, and legal and collective challenges to local and central government policy have developed with increasing frequency and impact.

In recent discussions and developments in this field, two main approaches to participation can be identified (Beresford, 1988; Pfeiffer and Coote, 1991). These can most helpfully be characterised as the 'consumerist' and the 'democratic' approaches. Although there are some overlaps between them, they reflect different, often competing, philosophies and objectives. The consumerist approach has been associated with the politics of the political 'new right', and the democratic approach with the emergence of disabled people's, self-advocacy, service users' and rights organisations and movements.

Both these approaches have strengths, but it is important not to confuse them. The emergence of consumerist thinking on health and welfare services coincided with the expansion of commercial provision and political pressure for a changed economy of welfare, placing much more emphasis on the market and exchange relations and much less on state provision. It conceives of service users or clients as 'customers' or 'consumers'. It overlays the idea of participation with the language of consumerism and the concerns of the market. Consumerism starts with the idea of buying goods and services rather than making collective provision for them. Two competing messages underpin the idea of consumerism: first, giving priority to the wants and needs of the 'consumer' and, second, framing people as consumers and 'commodifying' their needs (ie converting these needs into markets to be met by the creation and supply of goods and services).

The democratic approach to participation is much more clearly concerned with power and its redistribution and with people on the receiving end of social care and social services having more control over their lives and over agencies that intervene in them. This approach is concerned with how people are treated generally in mainstream society: with the achievement of people's civil and human rights, with challenging discrimination and oppression and with equality of opportunities and outcomes. These objectives have so far been most clearly and effectively pursued by the disabled people's movement and are closely reflected in the priority it has given in its campaigning to civil rights and anti-discrimination legislation, freedom of information legislation, and increased funding and support for organisations controlled by disabled people themselves.

While, as we have said, the democratic approach to participation has developed from the movements of disabled people, psychiatric system survivors and other users of social care services, the approach adopted by the service system and its proponents has predominantly been a consumerist one. Participation in social work and social services had been constructed primarily in terms of *services*, as 'user involvement'. In the UK, most such developments have been concerned with service users' participation in the planning and management of social services and health policy and provision. This has been the central focus of agency- and state-sponsored initiatives for involvement in social care and is where most effort and resources have gone. This has clearly been linked with the service system's own understandable interest in itself and broader concerns to improve its operation. Such initiatives for user involvement have mainly been concerned with obtaining data and intelligence for the service system, without any shift in the locus of decision making or redistribution of power. It has been reflected in a preponderance of information gathering and consultative exercises based on a consumerist approach to participation.

However, both the experience of service users and their organisations and conventional research suggest that the gains from this focus on involvement in service planning and management for service users and their organisations have been very limited. This was the finding from Bewley and Glendinning's study of involving disabled people in community care planning. They also found that there was a failure to include black people and minority ethnic groups effectively (Bewley and Glendinning, 1994). Such involvement in agency-led initiatives has generally required much effort for very limited change. The experience of getting involved is frequently negative and disempowering.

The service system in its planning and management has shown a remarkable capacity to resist the demands of its users expressed through consultation and conventional schemes for involvement. Peter Campbell's conclusion from the perspective of the psychiatric system survivors' movement has much broader relevance:

> Talk about tokenism and co-option has been frequent since the end of the 1980s, yet it is only recently that groups have started to turn down invitations to involvement. (Campbell, 1996, p 223)

Participation and older people

Different groups raise different issues for participation. These include, for example, issues of physical access and communication for disabled and deaf people; of anti-racism, interpretation and cultural sensitivity for black and minority ethnic groups; and of safe, supportive and non-threatening methods and environments for users of mental health services. Particular issues that have been identified in relation to older people's participation in the UK include generally lower levels of expectations, a frequent sense among them that they should be self-reliant and a reluctance to make demands. This is reflected in lower levels of participation, lower demands and low levels of take-up for some means-tested benefits (Beresford and Croft, 1978)

But this is only part of the picture. People in their 80s and beyond can and do get involved in participatory initiatives (Croft and Beresford, 1990). Many of the new approaches to participation that have been pioneered in recent years are helpful for the involvement and empowerment of older people (Beresford and Croft, 1993; Birkett, 1996). Sensitive approaches to involving older people in different policy areas (eg in housing) offer helpful insights and examples (Riseborough, 1996). There has also long been a large movement of older people, with local, regional, national and international organisations. This has developed its own campaigns, produced its own journals and newsletters, organised its own conferences and developed its own ethos and philosophy. In the UK, this movement has now begun to move beyond traditional concerns with income and pensions issues, to a broader focus that includes issues of social care and personal support. There is also an increasing awareness of the issues and rights of older people in the disabled people's movement, linked with the recognition that older people are the largest group experiencing disability in society. Older people and their organisations are also linking up with other social care service users' groups and movements to develop participatory schemes in association with them.

Whilst older people make up the largest group of users of social care services, arrangements and schemes for user involvement have tended to be least developed for this group, although the particular oppression they face through ageism highlights its particular importance for them. There have been fewer initiatives to involve them than other groups and they have been slower to develop. During the 1990s there has been an increased awareness and interest in the involvement of older people in social care. However, 'user involvement' for older people has tended to mirror user involvement more generally in social care. Agency initiatives have focused mainly on involvement in the planning and management of services (Thornton and Tozer, 1994, 1995; Tozer, 1995). They have also often not been inclusive. For example, the frequently cited Fife Users Panel Project, which sought to involve 'frail older people', did not include older people with dementia.

Agency-led approaches to participation based on user involvement in policy and service planning and management have not only resulted in limited change at broader macro levels. They have also frequently had a very limited impact at micro level in actually improving individual service users' lives and experience of services. They have generally remained distant and unconnected from service users' day-to-day experience. Ironically, service users who are drawn into agency-led schemes for user involvement that are meant to improve provision frequently experience minimal improvements in their own lives; they continue to live in poverty, without adequate support and with restricted choices and opportunities, even as they take part in such participatory initiatives. This applies to such schemes for older people no less than for other groups.

An alternative approach to participation

The agency-led approach to participation does not offer a firm basis for preventing or challenging elder abuse and is unlikely to have much impact on it, even though the information it offers may highlight the problem and place it more firmly on official agendas. A more helpful approach to participation in the context of elder abuse comes from service users and their organisations. This approach to involvement also shows more signs of success generally than that tied to the organisation and management of social services. Service users and their organisations have shown a growing distrust of and reluctance to get involved in traditional agency-led initiatives for their involvement in service and policy planning and management. Instead they are increasingly developing their own initiatives. They are now operating at two different but interrelated levels, linking the personal and the political. This approach combines a commitment to collective action and to the rights and needs of the individual. It is reflected both in broader campaigning, for example for accessible public transport and inclusive education, and in work for service users' increasing use of the law to secure their individual and collective rights. It is also highlighted by the increasing emphasis among service users' organisations on people being involved in defining, shaping and controlling the support they want and receive. This follows from the priority that disabled people's and service users' organisations give to making direct changes in their members' lives. Their primary concern is not the service system but improving their own and their peers' lives. This focus also means that they can avoid social services' own increasing preoccupation with organisational structure and managerialism.

In the UK, the growing concern of the disabled people's and service users' movements on people's involvement in their individual and personal experience of social work and social services is reflected in two developments. The first of these is the increasing focus that the movements are placing on extending people's control and involvement in social services and social care *practice*. There are a growing number of expressions of this development; these include service users' involvement in defining and developing standards for professional practice (Harding and Beresford, 1996) and in the definition and measurement of outcomes for social care. The Shaping Our Lives Project, a user-controlled initiative, offers an important example of the latter (Beresford et al, 1997; Shaping Our Lives Project, 1997; Turner, 1997a, b). Service users are also playing an increasing part in the establishment of a General Social Services Council to monitor and regulate social services practice. They are making clear that they want a real say in such a regulatory body: it must support service users to have more control over their lives and be guided by them both in recognising standards and skills and in safeguarding them (Brand, 1997).

The second and perhaps most innovative development in personal social services is the creation of direct payments schemes, embodied in the Community Care (Direct Payments) Act 1996. Research findings show that direct payment is a practicable, cost-effective policy option that is greatly preferred by service users who have been offered the choice (Oliver and Zarb, 1992; Morris, 1993). Such schemes, pioneered by the disabled people's movement as a way of making possible independent living, have been interpreted in consumerist terms by UK government. Some disabled people, including some psychiatric system survivors/mental health service users and some people with learning difficulties (although as yet not people aged 65 and over), are now permitted, as individual consumers, to purchase services directly as they choose instead of, as previously with the UK community care reforms, with the local authority acting as purchaser and care managers acting as assessors. The disabled people's movement, however, has developed a model for direct payments that goes far beyond consumerism. It is based on self-definition of need, rather than professional assessment, and on disabled people's organisations providing support, expertise, training and independent information and advocacy to enable service users to set up and run their own schemes for independent living.

These two interlinked aspects of the disabled people's and service users' movements' approach to participation, emphasising collective action and people regaining control over their lives, provide a helpful basis for countering elder abuse. This becomes clearer once we focus on the three key components, identified earlier, for challenging elder abuse and the inequalities of power associated with it: voice, choice and credibility.

Voice, choice and credibility

Supporting older people's voice, choice and credibility, all of which are severely restricted in the UK and western societies more generally, is central to challenging and preventing elder abuse, as can be seen if we look at the three more closely.

'Voice' means that people have ready access to effective and appropriate ways of saying what they want, articulate what is happening and reporting if there are difficulties or problems. It must mean that they have reliable and permanent lines of communication that can get past the closed doors of both domestic and institutional settings where they may be exposed to abuse, plus whatever support they need to make this a reality.

'Choice' means that people are in a position to make informed choices and for these to be acted upon; for them to know what is possible; and what the potential advantages and disadvantages of different courses of action may be. They are ensured access to whatever independent information this might require and given the opportunity to work out their decisions safely and at their own pace. They will be supported to make their own decisions, unless there is strong evidence that this is not possible, so that they are never faced with unacceptable options such as staying in abusive situations or going into residential institutions against their will. Supporting choice means building people's confidence and self-esteem, and ensuring that they can trust support services to act in accordance with their wants and preferences.

'Credibility' means that older people's views and perspectives must be accorded the validity due to them. It is not sufficient for older people to be able to express their views. These must also be valued and respected, listened to and acted upon. The views of social care service users generally and older people specifically are widely devalued. This is true of their views whether expressed collectively (Beresford and Campbell, 1994) or individually, and seems to be related both to broader ageist oppression and to the particular nature and history of the social care service system. As Chris Jones has said, social work and social services discourse has reinforced negative views of service users' capacity, generally seeing them in negative and deficit terms:

> It is a somewhat sobering experience analysing social work education and its knowledge base. For, in its mainstream at least, historical exploration of the past 100 years reveals startling continuities, such as social work's construction of clients as generally unworthy and manipulative individuals. Such a construction has contributed to a tragic legacy whereby clients are too often disregarded, not listened to and generally presented as people who don't count. This in turn must contribute to the episodes of cruelty and inhumanity which are periodically exposed. One cannot but wonder about the impact of mainstream social work's construction of clients on this 'writing off' of vulnerable people. (Jones, 1996, p 197)

Lessons from child abuse

Recent experience with child abuse offers a helpful route into understanding the importance of the three components of voice, choice and credibility. There has been growing interest in the field of elder abuse in seeing what lessons can be learned from child 'protection' and child abuse (eg Stevenson, 1996a, b), So far, increased participation has not been seen as having any particular significance. Indeed, one report discussed the involvement of older people who are thought to have been abused only in the context of case conferences and meetings and then concluded that their involvement was 'problematic' (Stevenson, 1996a, p 27). But this is perhaps not surprising in view of the fact that even the report of the National Commission of Inquiry into the Prevention of Child Abuse did not call for the increased participation of children and young people in its recommendations (King, 1997). This failure seems to be linked with the long tradition in personal social services of not giving priority to or including the views of service users.

Nevertheless, current and recent cases of institutionalised abuse in government 'care', ranging from the Staffordshire 'pin-down' affair to large-scale organised sexual abuse in local authority children's homes, have highlighted that children and young people have great difficulty in getting their voice heard; that even when they struggle to do so, they are frequently ignored or not believed; and that they frequently have little information or support, at least initially, with which to challenge abuse effectively.

Preventing and challenging elder abuse: a participatory strategy

Traditional social administration approaches seem unlikely to make much progress on advancing the voice, choice and credibility of older people, any more than they have done so far for those of children and young people. By contrast, the disabled people's and service users' movements' democratic and rights-based approach to participation offers a much more promising basis for increasing older people's voice, choice and credibility. It is also the approach that most closely connects with the growing recognition in professional discussion of elder abuse as a human rights issue, linked with broader issues of ageism, oppression, inequalities of power, difference and social division (eg Biggs and Phillipson, 1992; Social Services Inspectorate, 1992; George, 1994; Biggs et al, 1995; Aitken and Griffin, 1996, pp 155–156).

Supporting collective action

The emphasis of these movements on collective action provides a basis for the empowerment of older people, to which there is a growing commitment in both government and professional discussions of elder abuse (Biggs and Phillipson, 1992; Social Services Inspectorate, 1994). Whilst members of the disabled people's movement do not deny that there are individual as well as collective aspects to the process of empowerment, collective action is widely seen as the key to personal empowerment (Oliver, 1996, pp 147–148). The collective action of older people through self-advocacy, campaigning and mutual aid organisations also makes it possible:

- for older people to have their own discussions about elder abuse;
- to develop effective policies and practice for both collective and individual self, peer and professional advocacy;
- for older people to develop their own proposals and agenda for preventing and challenging elder abuse;
- to extend elder equality training provided by user trainers, both to support anti-oppressive policy and practice and to counter elder abuse;
- to develop and provide older people's own alternative services and support;
- for older people to ensure that their knowledge and experience are fully and centrally included in discussion;
- for older people to undertake their own monitoring, evaluation and research of elder abuse.

Some of these objectives are already being identified in professional discussions about elder abuse. For example, older people are beginning to make their own contributions to mainstream discussions about elder abuse (Lewisham Older Women's Network and the SAVE Project, 1995; SAVE Project, 1996); older people are being involved in undertaking research (Tozer and Thornton, 1995); and there is discussion of the importance of advocacy in challenging elder abuse. Citizen advocacy was pioneered in the USA and developed first with people with learning difficulties. However, using this approach for older people (Wolf, 1994, p 15; Biggs et al, 1995, p 108) is unlikely to have a major impact on elder abuse because the problems in developing more than a small-scale service, owing to its reliance on volunteers, remain unresolved. Chris Phillipson (1994, p 24) identifies the development of advocacy programmes and support for collective action as key strategies for empowering older people. But older people's collective action also offers the basis for a coherent and strategic approach to elder abuse. Moreover, it is the most effective way of advancing self-advocacy, which is now increasingly recognised as key to tackling the problem.

User involvement in professional practice

Increased participation in professional practice offers a crucial way of preventing and challenging elder abuse in both institutional and domestic settings. First, it can increase users' control over the services and support they receive, thus ensuring that these do not illegitimately restrict or infringe their rights. Second, it makes it possible for older people to reshape practice so that it reflects their, rather than professionals', priorities and concerns. Such participation can be achieved directly through direct payment schemes – which older people and their organisations are still struggling to access, having so far been excluded by legislation – and through greater involvement in standard setting, defining outcomes, monitoring and evaluating practice.

A holistic approach for the future

The identification of elder abuse as a social problem reflects rising concern for the rights and needs of older people. However, there is a danger, at a time of increased service rationing and political emphasis on making individual rather than collective provision to meet the needs of old age, that 'elder abuse' is separated from its broader socio-economic and political relations and that increasingly residualised public services are restricted to older people seen as the most vulnerable and most at risk of abuse. Already, as political and public expenditure priorities have changed, older people have increasingly been forced into dependency and socially excluded. There is now growing awareness of the need for a radical shift in policy and practice to support the independence and social inclusion of older people (Harding, 1997). Policy and practice on elder abuse that give priority to voice, choice and credibility and which fully involve older people and their organisations not only offer the prospect of making inroads into elder abuse but also ensure that it is connected with and part of a broader strategy for securing the rights and independence of older people.

Elder abuse and professional intervention: a social welfare model?

Mervyn Eastman

This chapter is a very personal reflection on the direction social work is taking as our understanding of elder abuse increases. It is personal because there is no single, easy road, no quick solution or blueprint against which to measure practice or even outcomes. Guidance from the Association of Directors of Social Services (1995) and from the Department of Health (1992) are offered as 'discussions'; they are not quite ready to nail their colours to the mast. Thus the cliché of 'crossroads' seems apt, and it may be timely to evaluate the responses of social services departments and to be aware of and sensitive to the flow from third and fourth generation writers and thinkers on elder abuse.

During 1996, two conferences were organised by the Age Concern Institute of Gerontology, in association with the Social Services Inspectorate and the Association of Directors of Social Services. The twin aims of the conferences were, first, to share the results of extensive cataloguing and evaluation of research (McCreadie, 1996a) and, secondly, to publicise an important paper on the significance of child protection experience for the emerging question of elder abuse (Stevenson, 1996a). Both documents were published in abridged form as part of the conference proceedings (McCreadie, 1996b).

These conferences, like so many others, raised more questions than they gave answers and highlighted two particular problems faced by practitioners. First, there is still no common definition of what we mean by 'elder abuse' and, second, research does not provide consistency of conclusion(s) – it remains contradictory and thus conflicting.

The field of elder abuse is in desperate need of practice-based material, tested and evaluated from both practitioners' and users' perspectives, promoting greater clarity about the roles and responsibilities of each stakeholder, be it social services, the medical profession or the police. This chapter is both a discussion and a debate, and I need to make clear the anxiety I have and to make explicit my own mindset. Are social care agencies, social services departments in particular, becoming the lead agency by default in the investigation of elder abuse and the protection of its victims? I do not believe it is a role or responsibility that should be given to or taken or accepted by local authorities.

The warnings provided by our experience of child protection (Parton, 1985, 1995) should act as beacons for those of us engaged in understanding elder abuse, but more especially those of us responsible for social care practice and its management. Textbooks, training manuals and research papers are one thing, but how does a social worker sitting in somebody's living-room actually confront the family or intervene effectively when abuse is suspected? Should that worker even be expected to confront them? Is it that worker's role to investigate or assess the risks? What protection do guidelines and protocols give to a home care worker who witnesses that abuse first-hand? Training modules, guidelines and case conferences can unwittingly seduce the participants and agency into believing their own rhetoric, underestimating the complexity and ambiguity of risk assessment intervention.

I offer a view, a position and an approach that move us away from investigations, protection and risk assessments towards constructing a model (or models) of response founded on and around existing networks and community-based care. I question the present general direction of social care and hope to illustrate an alternative approach specifically related to elder abuse. Without at least considering an alternative approach and direction, social services departments may find themselves over the next few years with a statutory requirement to protect older people, and we will have learned nothing from our experience of child care over the past 20 years. I am arguing for a system in which police officers investigate, the medical profession diagnoses and treats, and social care agencies focus on prevention and family/community support. Simplistic perhaps, but let us at least have the debate!

Nigel Parton, speaking at an important Child Protection Co-ordinators' Symposium, stated that in 'the harsh realities of the current situation ... social services child care is de facto child protection work' (Parton, 1995, p 13). This should be both a message and a warning for those of us interested in elder abuse, particularly as regards defining our role and tasks in relation to it. Do we really wish to see the support of older people become elder protection work surrounded and underpinned (even overwhelmed) by guidance, where each agency seeks to protect itself from public or ministerial blame when an older person is not protected?

The reader is invited to share the debate in this chapter (and indeed throughout this whole book). I am not asking for agreement but at least for consideration of an alternative role for social services.

'Messages from research'?

I have often said that it is relatively easy to be an expert in the field of elder abuse. Currently, one only needs to familiarise oneself with Claudine McCreadie's *Elder Abuse: Update on research* (1996a) to join the ranks of today's thinkers! McCreadie herself continues to show an earthly pragmatism and brings to her material a competence and humility rare among leading academics. Research and the conclusions that flow from it need to be treated with both caution and respect, because 'every researcher builds on the work of others, no matter how imperfect it may be ... we should all be able to learn from our own and others' mistakes' (Black, 1993, quoted in McCreadie, 1996a, p v). It is with that mindset that I approach all research, both my own and others.

What, then, are some of Stevenson's (1996b) key tentative conclusions from the present research field?

- Defining 'elder abuse' remains a difficult area.
- We need to avoid generalisations about abuse in domestic settings (distinguishing between different types of abuse, recognising that dependency or mental incapacity may not be so important as previously assumed, and in particular acknowledging powerful evidence that carer stress alone is not the principal reason for abuse).
- Little is known about abuse in residential care settings.
- There is considerable scope for financial abuse to occur.
- A policy for the protection of vulnerable adults is not the same as a policy on elder abuse: it is essential that agencies work together with skilled assessment that targets both parties in the abusive relationship.

It is important to note that multi-agency co-operation is seen to be key in addressing elder abuse. 'Working together', for those readers familiar with child protection, is a well worn and advocated path. Likewise, Black's comment reminds all of us that we build on each other's work, and tearing it to shreds runs counter to the spirit of working together.

Returning to the Age Concern conferences mentioned earlier, four overriding concerns were raised by participants: awareness, values, inter-agency working and support for good practice (McCreadie, 1996b, pp 28ff). Of particular interest for our present discussion were: first, that elder abuse should be viewed in the wider context of *welfare and the well-being of older people* (my emphasis); secondly, the danger of uncritically reproducing child protection models, with their essentially paternalistic approaches; thirdly, the problems associated with single agencies (notably social services departments) working in isolation; and finally, the danger of excessive 'proceduralisation', and the need for flexibility. For the purpose of this contribution, such messages were particularly encouraging, coming as they did from the floor not the platform! They each have a resonance here as we take the debate forward in the direction of social care interventions and practice.

In her comparison of elder abuse with child protection, Stevenson (1996b) summarised eight areas of similarities, differences and issues of particular interest to us:

- the impact of 'proceduralisation' on policy and practice;
- the dominance of the risk model;
- the tension between the interests of the parties involved;
- the impact of research on policy and practice;
- present trends towards increased family support;
- inter-agency co-operation;
- the involvement of 'caretakers' in the protective process;
- logically distinguishing specific categories of abuse.

Stevenson argued that social care must be alert to excessive protection procedures: child protection and the dominance of risk factors have placed workers in a vulnerable and ambiguous position because this approach may suggest a spurious certainty. She continued by emphasising that the 'welfare' model is likely to contribute more to the protection of older people than a concentration on risk; 'welfare' also fits better with notions of community care. Finally, effective communication and co-operation between agencies will not be achieved without an element of 'proceduralisation' and integrated training concerning common social values.

We therefore begin to see some early indicators of warning from notable and credible researchers who have looked into elder abuse. We must also explore the thinking of *Child Protection: Messages from research* (Department of Health, 1995) and the very useful perspective of Nigel Parton (1995). In essence, *Messages from research* highlighted the fact that the criteria legitimising social services intervention are predominantly concerned with the protection of high-risk children. Thus, in the absence of a clear nation-wide definition, how an agency defines abuse locally will create a somewhat subjective, moral and arbitrary boundary between older people, their carers who experience state intervention and those who do not. Who interprets? Who decides the effectiveness of any outcome?

A second message, of relevance to our debate here, was that families caught up in the child protection process are generally multiply disadvantaged. The process does in fact ensure that 95 per cent of children remain at home and the majority of those separated are swiftly reunited. As local authorities are encouraged to provide guidance and protocols on elder abuse, is there a danger that the processes underpinning the guidance will force older people and their families to experience control by the state, the vast majority of older people at risk (or not, depending on who's doing the risk analysis) finding themselves stigmatised, labelled and completely powerless? Too often an initial enquiry or referral becomes an investigation, and support is somewhat incidental. An agency becoming involved with a child or family does not mean that the family will receive or even be offered support. As long as the procedure has been followed, the agency has 'protected' itself. This is all well and good, but surely not an adequate response.

A final message is that professionals are often far less concerned with the way families are left when the enquiry is completed and concerns subside than they are with the way children enter the protection process. Children, older people and their families are left to pick up the pieces as the social services departments are forced to turn their attention and resources to the next risk assessment and initial enquiry!

One last word at this juncture. *Messages from research* (Department of Health, 1995) was and is an extremely important document, and a startling and disturbing message to those of us in social services. We are often preoccupied with a particular incident or event and are forced to ignore the wider context, choosing the wrong 'career avenue' for the child and/or excluding the family from the enquiry. The message for elder abuse cannot be clearer – we must be wary of taking on the lead role of investigation and risk assessment.

Let us turn to Parton (1995) to consolidate the message thus far. Parton began to feel uneasy about the rather simplistic and straightforward approach of guidelines and training in child protection, set against the complexities and contradictions that faced social workers and their managers. He was not convinced that policies and procedures were 'as humane as was assumed'. The conclusion to *The Politics of Child Abuse* posed two scenarios: in one, policy will be driven by partnership, prevention and family support; alternatively, policy will be driven by investigation and protection, and welfare/support models will be sacrificed on the altar of risk assessment.

Despite appearances to the contrary, the driving force behind children's legislation, including the Children Act 1989, was (and remains) a concern with protection, not broader considerations of child welfare. Parton argues that the dominance of child protection is having 'very deleterious outcomes, particularly for the children and families involved' (Parton, 1995, p 3). At a time when we are expecting legislation pursuant to the Green Paper on mental incapacity (Lord Chancellor's Department, 1997), let us take heed lest the resultant legislation is underpinned by the dominant theme of protection!

Parton, rightly in my view, characterises contemporary child protection work as the need to identify 'high risk' in a context where joint working is set out in increasingly complex yet specific procedural guidelines and intervention framed by a narrow emphasis on legislation and the need for forensic evidence. Where are the understanding, recognition and case conference strategies that reflect social exclusion, housing shortages, social isolation, resource reductions, changes in local government management, health care reforms and legislation in relation to schools? (Parton, 1995, p 3)

This is not the place to rehearse or detail the fuller arguments used by Parton. Let it be sufficient, though, to alert those of us in the field of elder abuse to take a breath, not to simply and without thought accept the protection model of intervention. Neither should we assume that multi-agency, joint working and procedural guidelines alone will address the ambiguities and complexities faced by front-line social and health care professionals.

'Doctor! Doctor!'

Whilst there is no disagreement about the need to ensure effective collaboration between different professionals, we must look now at the influence clinicians have had on our understanding of elder abuse – and especially at the so-called 'medical' model underpinning policy and intervention being increasingly adopted by social services depart- ments. At the Age Concern Institute of Gerontology conferences (where the majority of those attending were from non-health back- grounds) doubt was expressed about 'medicalising' the issue of elder abuse (McCreadie, 1996b, p 29). What is it that causes non-health practitioners and managers to feel uneasy? When we refer to 'medical' versus 'social' care models, what do we actually mean?

In the UK, it is arguably the medical profession who led the first- generation writers on elder abuse (Baker, 1975; Burston, 1975). They received little professional or public attention. The term 'granny bat- tering' was more a reflection of journalistic sensationalism than an analytical concept coined by the authors themselves. It was probably the 1988 British Geriatric Society's multi-agency conference in Lon- don (Tomlin, 1989) that acted as a catalyst and trigger for the medical profession.

Notwithstanding the excellent contributions of authors of the calibre of Elizabeth Hocking, dating back to the early 1980s (see Eastman, 1994, pp 51ff, for details), Gerry Bennett and his associates have with- out doubt become the leading clinicians among later generations of researchers and writers. His influence, particularly via Action on Elder Abuse, has contributed significantly to framing our view of elder abuse in terms of its conceptualisation and how agencies shall respond. That contribution should be neither underestimated nor discounted.

Yet the 'discovery' of elder abuse could already be seen to be follow- ing child care/protection patterns. The prevailing model is that of diagnosis and treatment, which could be seen to be paternalistic ('we know best'). We 'understand' abuse by characterising and categorising the abusers, the victims and the risk, seeking to unearth uniform man- ifestations that might lead to robust diagnoses and reliable prognoses. A medical model will in essence seek to predict, categorise, diagnose and then treat. The diagnosis rests on actual psychological or physio- logical signs of abuse, collecting evidence of episodes of abuse but not acting as a reliable predictor of future activity. Social services may be left to take that last responsibility. The problem is that the model excludes or pays lip service to the wider context of social exclusion, social control, isolation and the 'social construction of ageing' (Phillipson, 1982).

Is there an argument here that says the medical model legitimises the role of social care professionals? The medical profession, the real 'experts', defines essential terms of reference and then passes responsibility to social services to 'do something' (Parton, 1985, p 149). Is this one step away from an agency being given responsibility for predicting families at risk, investigating alleged incidents, assessing risk and then finally being charged with a statutory responsibility to protect vulnerable adults?

Turning now to models of intervention, Bennett and Kingston (1993) helpfully outlined a continuum ranging from 'passive' to 'aggressive', allowing for subtle gradations along the way. In addition, they discussed the control–compassion spectrum, ranging from control underpinned by legal remedies (removal, prosecution, supervision orders) to compassion (family support, day care). These models support the notion that both abuser and abused are victims. Bennett and Kingston, while questioning Eastman's (1984) view that the stress of caring is a key factor, nevertheless point out that in future 'we need to differentiate between different causative factors and intervene appropriately'. Indeed, they concede that 'stressed caregivers may require support and service provision to reduce stressors' (Bennett and Kingston, 1993, p 53). 'Pathological abusers', by contrast, require legal intervention. But what is a pathological abuser? Can it be that the human action is being categorised and made comparable to a natural organism and therefore determined and caused by objective factors?

Adapting a Partonian quote (1995, p 147) to the elder abuse context, one might say that 'the study of elder abuse is reduced to the examination of antecedent factors, or their indicators and correlates'. If we can then stop or modify the antecedent factor, we may be able to stop or modify the problem. The unease of non-health workers at this prospect may well reflect the problematical nature of identification, predictability and protection/prevention. It is assumed that abusers of older people are influenced by defined factors or causes whereby the focus is on the abusers and by studying them we will be able to explain the incidence, nature and prevalence of elder abuse.

Existing guidelines introduced by local authority social services departments, sometimes in collaboration with health authorities and trusts and occasionally with police co-operation, place a heavy emphasis on investigation, defining the nature of the alleged abuse and determinants of risk. Such guidance and procedures are firmly based in a model of incidence, predictability and protection. The social worker or care manager is then left to offer support that minimises or stops the abuse.

As with child protection, welfare agencies are in danger of being given or willingly taking 'the responsibility for solving problems which lie well beyond their remit' (Parton, 1985, p 7). There is also a danger that government departments or even ministers will see the protection of older people, especially those in institutions, as being ensured by social services departments exercising their regulatory function and responsibility and/or setting standards and monitoring contracts. It is my contention that procedure-led intervention will neither protect nor support older people and their families, nor will it confront the complexities inherent in so-called abusive families, organisational culture or institutions.

Back to welfare?

The arguments advanced by Parton and others (eg Holman, 1993) are of the utmost significance. The debate concerns the effectiveness not only of child care but also of the basic policies and practices behind the community care reforms. As community care underpins our work in relation to older people we need to examine these concerns. Community care legislation has pervaded social work and care with its purchaser/provider contract culture based on particular values and assumptions about individuals, groups and the state, and about appropriate relations among them. Even in 1985 Parton highlighted that this approach in child care policy and practice had proved significantly unsuccessful in eliminating child abuse or deaths. In essence, the belief that, through control or coercion, agencies can be effective in confronting abuse has to be challenged.

Social workers have repeatedly been held responsible for failing to control abusers and/or doubly damned if risk factors were misinterpreted and thus the interventions proved unsuccessful. Welfare was, and still is, perceived by some as somewhat soft, wet, intellectual or even 'inherently evil' (Holman, 1993). The community care legislation governing how social services departments work with older people was underpinned by very crude assumptions: state welfare had fed the 'fecklessness' of parents, especially women who neglected their children and caused those children to become 'delinquent layabouts' (Holman, 1993, p 15).

The state, by adopting a commissioner role and thus purchasing support and care from independent or private care providers, was to become more efficient. This, I believe, furthered and actually institutionalised the development of social welfare being provided by non-local authority agencies, with social services work limited to the assessment of eligibility and risk and co-ordinating care packages. This direction has had a significant impact on how we think about assessment, care management and supportive service provision and intervention.

Such a shift from local authority provision suited the medical model very well. The contract culture has squeezed social work and welfare into increasingly prescriptive and narrow lines. Elder abuse will, I fear, become just another issue that is categorised, labelled and pigeonholed. Social workers and health professionals with checklists and procedures (processes) will predict risk, determine eligibility and then commission and purchase support services from the independent sector. The care management function will orchestrate the provision of services, but if a tragedy occurs it will be the commissioners and purchasers who will be held responsible. Enter the local authority's legal department (to protect the authority) and forensic medicine (to determine the evidence).

Our understanding of elder abuse is still fairly rudimentary and our responses to it vary enormously. The priority it is given is frequently more reliant on, and determined by, local champions than any coherent policy framework. As the Association of Directors of Social Services, Department of Health and voluntary organisations such as Action on

Elder Abuse and the newly formed Professional Alliance Against Abuse of Vulnerable Adults (PAAVA) seek to fill that policy vacuum, we must be mindful and sensitive to the models we use to frame our understanding of a problem and the consequent responses. In seeking to develop a welfare-based model, we need to look at Holman's (1993) critique of the belief systems underlying the reforms and what they have led to.

What then are the 'serious, adverse and regrettable' consequences of the past 18–20 years (Parton, 1995)? Translating them to the field of elder abuse they could be seen to be:

- The emphasis of 'management-speak' which has distanced social services managers from front-line staff as we seek to create out of social welfare 'a sharp, well-informed business' (Holman, 1993, p 32).
- Social welfare/work has become mechanistic, with an emphasis on procedures, protocols, form filling, at-risk registers and contract negotiations.
- Increased managerial control of front-line activity and reduced discretion as a result of 'proceduralisation'.
- Care management is not co-terminous with social work.
- Elder abuse work is characterised by control and coercion.
- Preventive interventions are marginalised because of the obsession with eligibility criteria to deal with costs rather than needs.
- Internal and external markets have created additional tiers of management hierarchy.
- Registration and inspection procedures have yet to demonstrate a significant impact on the level of abuse in residential settings (Valios, 1997).

The core point made by Parton to re-address the imbalance with regard to child welfare versus protection was to question the concept of multi-agency integration. He has put forward the notion that responsibilities, resources and lines of accountability should be separated and demarcated.

Holman (1993) has articulated a characteristically clear blueprint to deal with the tensions between prevention and protection in the modern contract culture. I am not advocating this approach; I simply apply it to the field of elder abuse by way of illustrating a different model based on community interventions that challenges existing models.

- The local authority becomes the main service provider accountable to the local population through the democratic process. Services should be properly funded.
- Social welfare staff working directly with elder abuse should support families, advocating on their behalf and seeking out resources that enable them to cope with their own lives.
- Services are based on the concept of community and neighbourhood, not on individual pathology (the 'abusers').
- Social welfare for older people should be located in local communities (day and residential centres offering a whole range of health and social support, accessible out of hours with adequate transport), and aiming above all to destigmatise elder abuse and to focus on prevention as opposed to investigation.
- Agencies should develop departmental, corporate and multi-disciplinary strategies to confront social exclusion, isolation, low levels of benefit take-up, etc.
- Social services departments should strengthen the activity of existing users and community groups.
- Local authority social care should be based on the concept of mutual obligations towards each other, common kinship and joint action.

In essence, we could argue that existing eligibility criteria should be turned on their head: individuals and families currently classified as medium/low need should be acknowledged as most deserving of and responsive to our services, while those known to be abusing would enter an entirely different service construction and response. Such a scenario is highly unlikely, of course, but at least it offers a provocative reminder of the preventive thrust of section 45 of the Health Services and Public Health Act 1968, which is still in force.

Aitken and Griffin (1996) challenge existing frameworks that ignore gender/sexist and age/ageist issues, and particularly the relationship between the two. Their thesis is that elder abuse violates the 1948 Universal Declaration of Human Rights, in particular the 'inalienable right to freedom from fear and want, and the equal rights of men and women' (quoted in Aitken and Griffin, 1996, p 156). This dovetails conveniently with the underlying principle that personal experience should form the basis of both theory and practice: 'experience, theory and practice should exist in mutual and immediate relationship with each other' (Stanley and Wise, 1993, p 89).   ·

Conclusion

Social welfare, not protection, should be the focus of social services activity. We should not, either by our actions or by default, become the lead elder abuse protection agency. Services should be community based and organised around local community groups. Meanwhile, investigation and initial assessment of suspected elder abuse should be undertaken by an agency entirely different and separate from social services. Such a scenario will not become reality without a fundamental reconstruction of social care.

In addition, we need to challenge and confront existing ageist and sexist constructions to existing service provision. Front-line staff and their managers, in partnership with users and local communities, should set the agenda, design the service responses and ensure that local people determine how those services are organised and delivered. Social welfare is about the empowerment of users, not control. Genuine empowerment requires well-funded, locally accountable responses that destigmatise both 'abusers' and 'abused'. Above all, we need to question the present elder abuse construction that will, if not challenged, straitjacket us in the arena of investigation, risk assessment and protection.

Elder abuse and social work: integrated learning at qualifying level

Phil Slater and Samia Naouar Ben Romdhane

Public recognition of a social problem is inevitably accompanied by an emphasis on the need for appropriate training. In the case of elder abuse, practice guidelines from the Department of Health have officially endorsed the vital importance of this dimension: 'both managers and staff must be helped to develop and update the skills appropriate to work in this area' (Department of Health, 1993, p 10).

Materials already on offer to meet this staff development need are many and various, ranging from discussions of the principles informing effective training (Biggs and Phillipson, 1994; Biggs et al, 1995; Zlotnick, 1995), through detailed accounts of training programmes (Pillemer and Hudson, 1993; Zlotnick, 1993; Goudie and Alcott, 1994; Keller, 1996), to off-the-peg training manuals themselves (Biggs and Phillipson, 1992; Pritchard, 1995, 1996). Comparative evaluation of these materials would be a useful exercise in itself. In the present context, however, the most significant factor is what they have in common, namely a predominant or even exclusive concern with in-house training of operational staff.

By way of contrast, a major campaigning document (Action on Elder Abuse, 1995) implies a broader spectrum of learning, repeatedly emphasising the need to develop 'systematic training and education', although the distinction between the two is not further elaborated in that text. This is partially remedied via an important article which, starting out from a perceived deficiency in detection and intervention skills among medical and social work professionals, targets its research in accordance with a not unreasonable assumption: 'an obvious way to improve this apparently deficient position is to improve the knowledge base of the professionals involved, in particular at the level of their initial qualifying and registration courses' (Kingston et al, 1995, p 354).

With specific reference to social workers, the idea of including elder abuse learning in qualifying programmes might appear to be contradicted by the identification by the Central Council for Education and Training in Social Work (CCETSW) of 'working effectively in situations where they carry responsibility for those at serious risk, for example, in the areas of child/adult abuse' as one of the essential hallmarks of post-qualifying practice (CCETSW, 1992, p 15). This would be in line with the general thrust of related guidance on child protection work (Home Office et al, 1991) and with directions from the Secretary of State in respect of the appointment of approved social workers under the Mental Health Act (Department of Health and Social Security, 1986).

However, whilst there may be a clear case for restricting direct allocation of this type of work to social workers benefiting from post-qualifying developments, students on qualifying programmes could well encounter situations involving serious risk that have not yet been diagnosed as such. This is recognised in a contribution to CCETSW's 'Good Practice' series, which, in pursuit of 'quality work' with older people, argues the importance of students at qualifying level developing their understanding of elder abuse in general and of professional responses in particular, including the process of referring on to more experienced colleagues (Winner, 1992, pp 20ff).

The present chapter explores in depth the scope for incorporating learning about elder abuse into social work education at qualifying level. From the outset, the discussion will necessarily confront major theoretical complexities and serious organisational dilemmas. Nevertheless, the chapter presents a positive framework for the integration of learning about elder abuse in a rounded professional education. General considerations are illustrated by reference to a specific local network spanning the traditional divide between college-based theoretical learning and agency-based practice learning. Simultaneously, the subject matter is brought dramatically to life via extensive consideration of a case that materialised on this network. Highlighting the learning outcomes implicit in the case, the chapter concludes with a distillation of the implications for direct practice.

Qualifying curriculum

The pertinence of social work to the problem of elder abuse should be readily apparent from the following pronouncement.

> The purpose of social work is to enable children, adults, families, groups and communities to function, participate and develop in society. Social workers practise in a society of complexity, change and diversity, and the majority of people to whom they provide services are among the most vulnerable and disadvantaged in that society ... They have to balance the needs, rights, responsibilities and resources of people with those of the wider community, and provide appropriate levels of support, advocacy, care, protection and control. (CCETSW, 1995, p 16)

Given this general statement of the purpose of social work in the rules and requirements for qualifying programmes, it seems reasonable to ask (as in the title of the research article already cited) 'is elder abuse on the curriculum?' (Kingston et al, 1995). The survey by Kingston and colleagues of DipSW programmes answered the question in the affirmative by a ratio of 19 to 1. While this quantitative finding satisfied the article's central concern, semi-structured feedback from programme personnel also served to highlight two important organisational considerations: the relative size of specific inputs on elder abuse, and their location in any one programme.

These considerations echo the general problem of 'curriculum over-load', as formulated by the late Veronica Coulshed (1988, p 157). In a remarkably prescient article, she took issue with the process whereby a potentially infinite range of discrete social problems was imported into qualifying courses, usually in response to pressure from campaign groups (but not infrequently from students themselves) to 'please include something' on race, gender, domestic violence, HIV/AIDS, the purchaser/provider split, female genital mutilation, European employment prospects, or whatever. By adding 'a dash of this and a drop of that', professional education threatened to degenerate into a Cook's-style 'world tour' of subjects whose individual significance was not in question but whose meaning within an overall professional ambit was not so much non-transparent as non-existent.

Propounding the objective of a properly integrated curriculum, Coulshed went on to outline a spectrum of 'organising rubrics', ranging from methods of intervention (eg casework), through specific client groups (reflecting the terminological constructions of social policy), to the core skills related to social work's purpose and functions. The practical value of such an approach to curriculum design was not to impose imperious dictates but to accommodate reasonable (and explicitly reasoned) choices. It is interesting that victims of abuse and vulnerable elderly people were mentioned, not in the spirit of 'a dash of this and a drop of that' but under the organising rubric of client groupings. Thereby, incidentally, Coulshed touched on a major problem that was to confront the new wave of writers of elder abuse publications in the 1990s (Slater, 1996b). Amazingly, her article was published in 1988, and presumably written even earlier.

A year later, the cause of integrated curriculum development was significantly advanced by CCETSW. Exercising its powers under section 10 of the Health and Social Services and Social Security Adjudications Act 1983, it launched a multi-faceted framework for qualifying training (ie training that confers the status of 'qualified social worker'), implicitly endorsing the concept of 'organising rubrics', not merely in relation to the well-developed sphere of classroom teaching and written assignments but also extending to the previously neglected world of practice placement. The twin sets of regulations relating to these complementary dimensions went into revised (but not substantially modified) editions two years later (CCETSW, 1991a, b), to be superseded by three completely recast volumes in the current 'Assuring Quality' series (CCETSW, 1995, 1996a, b).

The essential components of this framework must be properly understood, both individually and in their mutual interdependence, if the scope for integrated social work learning about elder abuse in qualifying programmes is to be seriously explored.

DipSW requirements

The central pillar of the CCETSW's framework for qualifying training is the DipSW programme itself, located at higher education level and provided jointly by at least one educational institution and an associated practice agency. Learning outcomes are organised around a set of practice competences. In the current version, these are synthesised into six core competences, with official sanctioning of the following shorthand: communicate and engage; promote and enable; assess and plan; intervene and provide services; work in organisations; develop professional competence.

The organisation of social work teaching and learning around a set of vocational competences has been the subject of often heated debate, although the best contributions to the debate (Yelloly and Henkel, 1995) are admirably restrained in tone and considered in their judgement. In much the same spirit, the present chapter aims not to take up a dogmatic position for or against the competence focus as such, but to explore the scope for accommodating learning about elder abuse within the parameters of the DipSW programme as currently constituted.

In fact, one need look no further than the longhand formulation of the core competences to find suitable 'pegs'. Assessing and planning, for example, includes responses to 'need and risk' in general, while communicating and engaging makes specific reference to 'adults at risk'. Intervening and providing services refers to the provision and/or purchase of 'appropriate levels of support, care, protection and control'. So even at the most general level of the core competences, there is no shortage of scope for incorporating specific learning about elder abuse.

This scope is confirmed at the subsequent level of exposition, where each core competence is analysed into a set of practice requirements, each supplied with a range of evidence indicators. Most significantly in the present context, assessing and planning includes the practice requirement to 'work in partnership to identify and analyse risk of harm, abuse or failure to protect'. The evidence indicators (CCETSW, 1995, p 27) merit citation in full:

- Identify potential harm, abuse, neglect and failure to protect.
- Work in partnership to collate information about potential risk, harm, abuse, neglect or failure to protect.
- Analyse and evaluate risk of harm, neglect, abuse or failure to protect.
- Balance the rights of people to take risks against the likelihood of harm ensuing.
- Evaluate evidence for intervention on the basis of statutory requirements and organisational policy and procedures.

All in all, the CCETSW's formulation of core competences, practice requirements and evidence indicators clearly offers ample scope for accommodating teaching about elder abuse at qualifying level.

Given the genuine reservations that many professionals and educators have expressed about a narrowly defined competence focus, it seems only fair to add that this is not the full DipSW scenario. Common to all editions of the regulations has been the view that competence in social work is the 'product' of knowledge, skills and values. Indeed, as the latest edition is at pains to emphasise, practice can be described as competent only if it is 'founded on values, carried out in a skilled manner and informed by knowledge, critical analysis and reflection' (CCETSW, 1995, p 17).

Whilst the specific skills dimension is significantly underplayed in the current version, the other two components are elaborated in varying degrees. The officially stated knowledge base makes explicit reference to the 'range and impact of physical, social, sexual and emotional neglect and abuse' together with the 'concept of risk, the right to take risk, and management of risk' (CCETSW, 1995, pp 21ff). Formulated independently in terms of professional values, this entails a requirement to 'promote people's rights to choice, privacy, confidentiality and protection, while recognising and addressing the complexities of competing rights and demands' (CCETSW, 1995, p 18).

However, while such formulations offer ample justification for including elder abuse in college teaching available to all students, the DipSW framework simultaneously recognises the constraints imposed by a qualifying programme still restricted to two years. Mindful of the strictures on unrealistic expectations voiced in the first Blom-Cooper Report (London Borough of Brent, 1985), CCETSW's original launch of the DipSW regulations combined generic teaching of a common curriculum with specific demonstration of competence in an 'area of particular practice' (CCETSW, 1991b). This was subsequently replaced by the language of 'particular pathways', associated with particular services or settings, or work with particular service user groups (CCETSW, 1995).

By way of illustration, CCETSW offered the supposedly uncontentious distinction of probation, children/families and adult/community care pathways, but stopped short of being prescriptive, leaving it to the DipSW programmes themselves to decide how best to combine generic teaching inputs with 'deeper, more extensive understanding of knowledge particularly relevant to the service user group and context of their practice learning opportunities' (CCETSW, 1995, p 19). The college dimension of pathway learning in relation to elder abuse is considered in due course. For the moment, it is important to give some general consideration to the CCETSW's regulations in respect of practice learning, in order to establish the scope for specific learning about elder abuse.

Practice learning

It is a long-standing principle of social work qualifying training, first codified in the so-called Younghusband Report (Ministry of Health, 1959), that qualifying courses/programmes should actively promote the integration of theory and practice via complementary (ideally concurrent) college-based teaching and assessment, and agency-based supervised practice.

From 1989, the language of 'placement supervision' was superseded by the language of 'practice teaching' in a major CCETSW initiative to raise standards of practice generally and professional accountability in particular (Slater, 1996a). CCETSW's long-term (and as yet unfulfilled) aim was that all DipSW students should undertake their practice placements in 'approved' practice learning agencies, supervised by staff who were 'accredited practice teachers' in their agency (CCETSW, 1991a, p 8).

Transitional arrangements were made for the accreditation of existing placement supervisors with substantial up-to-date experience. For future generations of practice teachers, by contrast, accreditation would be available only on the basis of holding the newly created Practice Teaching Award, gained via assessment on a CCETSW-approved practice teacher programme. The first few generations of candidates for the Award were assessed against 14 requirements, including the ability to 'identify, develop and provide learning opportunities for students'; to 'help students to relate theory and practice'; and to 'supervise the student's practice as an accountable member of the agency's staff'.

The somewhat ambiguous formulation of the last requirement was improved on greatly when the original requirements for the Award were superseded under the auspices of the 'Assuring Quality' series (CCETSW, 1996b). Competence Element B3 reads: 'manage and monitor the student's practice and progress within the placement and safeguard the quality of service to and safety of users'. This serves to pinpoint a dilemma in relation to the specific issue of learning about elder abuse. How can DipSW students be provided with practice learning opportunities without compromising the primacy of considerations about users' safety? Fortunately, this is not a dilemma that practice teachers need face alone, and CCETSW offers a useful reminder in this regard, as follows. Over and above the significant initiatives already outlined in relation to the training, assessment and accreditation of practice teachers, 1989 also saw the launch of novel arrangements for CCETSW approval of practice learning agencies in their own right. Initially, agency approval was based on two criteria: first, a policy commitment to the provision of high quality practice learning opportunities, with special reference to anti-discriminatory practice; second, the existence of good systems for the support and guidance of practice teachers.

The latter criterion was elaborated to include systems of accountability for work undertaken by students as well as for 'the type and level of work which can be allocated to students, and any restrictions on it' (CCETSW, 1991a, pp 5ff). Such a perspective is doubly helpful: first, it emphasises that the provision of practice learning opportunities must always remain subordinate to considerations of duty of care towards service users; secondly, it acknowledges that such considerations are not solely the responsibility of practice teachers, accredited or otherwise, but are shared with the employing agency itself.

Obviously, an agency might be inclined to issue blanket bans on students having any involvement in cases where there is evidence or even suspicion of elder abuse. But Department of Health guidance is far more open-minded on this question:

> Some aspects of elder abuse work such as identification, assessment, counselling and care planning should be undertaken only by skilled, trained staff. Many others, often not professionally trained, will be involved at various times, and will be able to make a helpful contribution if they are given adequate training and support. (Department of Health, 1995, p 11)

Midway between these two extremes, DipSW students on practice placement would seem to constitute a third category of staff, not yet professionally qualified but currently undertaking such training, bolstered by CCETSW's arrangements for effective practice learning in tandem with classroom teaching.

The following case study offers a dramatic example both of the provision of a practice learning opportunity on the margins of elder abuse and, more tellingly, of necessary adjustments to the practice learning arrangements as elder abuse threatened to dominate the proceedings.

Introduction to case study

In moving from theoretical generalities to specific cases, one treads familiar territory in the history of social work education, and there is no reason to suspect that elder abuse will prove exceptional in this regard. Indeed, numerous authors have already recommended the use of case studies to promote learning among health and social services personnel (Biggs and Phillipson, 1992; Pritchard, 1995, 1996; Keller, 1996). One author has specifically recommended the use of 'live or imaginary case material' in relation to elder abuse as part of a simulated assessment task on DipSW programmes (Winner, 1992, p 21).

Live (as opposed to imaginary) case material is, of course, integral to the practice learning of DipSW students. As part of the placement agency's direct service provision, students are required, like their qualified colleagues, to account for their practice orally in formal supervision, and to supplement this in writing via a range of assessment, planning, review and termination/transfer reports. Additionally, DipSW assessment panels themselves require students to furnish evidence drawn from their practice of meeting the six core competences and applying the values requirements (CCETSW, 1995). In college, confidence in this task is promoted via the traditional facility of group tutorials, in which students are encouraged to share and reflect on live practice material.

In using real case studies, primary consideration must be given to the protection of clients' identities, although a simple change of surname usually suffices. In the present context, by contrast, where details of a case are to be disseminated via a published text, considerations of confidentiality are rather more complex. Interestingly, however, remarkably little has been written on how to maintain confidentiality when handling case studies. Given this state of affairs, it is in order to preface the presentation of the case in question with a few brief words by way of clarifying the authors' own confidentiality strategy.

Obviously, the foremost purpose is to guarantee complete anonymity. This requires not just the standard use of aliases but also refraining from any substantive statement that could lead to the identification of true identities by third parties. However, camouflaging the facts should not amount to a travesty of the facts pertaining to the essential components of people's identities. A gay black man, for example, should not transmogrify into a heterosexual white woman, any more than a Kurdish juvenile fleeing from persecution in Iraq should metamorphose into an Anglo-Saxon runaway from a home counties boarding school.

By the same token, the encoding of people's names should be in accordance with broadly based cultural patterns. Thus, an elderly woman named Mildred might be referred to as Ruby or Agnes, but not as Sharon or Olugumu. Likewise, country of origin might be shifted within a particular ethnic region, so that Barbados becomes Tobago, but not Sweden. In similar spirit, ages might be varied by a year or two, such that 71 is increased to 73, but not to the extent that 90 becomes 65. Finally, while professional nomenclature might well need some camouflaging ('domiciliary care worker' becoming 'home care worker', for example), the essential parameters of local services should be faithfully reproduced.

Transcribed in accordance with these principles, the case of 'Lucie Ziegler' can now be presented.

Lucie is a 68-year-old woman, originally from Czechoslovakia, who has lived in London since 1945. Her husband, Oskar, died of cancer in 1964, leaving her to raise a daughter, Maria, who maintains telephone contact from Wales. The house is owner-occupied, with no outstanding mortgage, but in a state of decorative disrepair although structurally sound. In addition to the standard state pension and a small personal pension, Lucie has savings of £30,000. For the past 25 years, she has lived with a Cornish man by the name of Arthur Wilson, who is a few months younger than Lucie. He originally moved in as a lodger, but for the past 15 years they have lived together as common law husband and wife.

Earlier this year, Lucie was referred to a psycho-geriatrician by the GP, who expressed concern about Lucie's mental deterioration and physical self-neglect, as well as the need to support Arthur in the role of carer. Follow-up consultation with the GP revealed that, although Lucie was a long-standing patient of his, the present concerns had been triggered by a referral from the local police. They had been called to the

home by Lucie, alleging that the weekly income, together with occasional withdrawals from her savings, were 'going missing'. The previous
day, when she had challenged Arthur on the subject, she had been
'slapped about' by him.

Visiting within hours of the call, two police officers had formed a view
of Lucie as extremely 'confused', apparently unaware of what day it
was and unable to give a coherent account of monetary transactions.
There were no visible signs of injuries to the face, and Lucie had
declined the suggestion of a full medical examination. For his part,
Arthur had vehemently denied any wrongdoing, and accused Lucie of
fabrication, out of a combination of 'trouble causing' and 'feeble mind-
edness'. This fitted with the police officers' assessment of Lucie as an
'unreliable witness', in need of some sort of medical and/or psychiatric
help, as opposed to further police investigation. Hence the referral to
the GP, who implicitly confirmed this assessment by referring on to the
psycho-geriatrician, whose constituency was people of pensionable
age with mental health problems.

The psychiatrist undertook a home visit, accompanied by a social
worker attached to the hospital-based multi-disciplinary team. Lucie
was implacably opposed to the suggestion of mental ill health, and
refused to consent to any sort of psychiatric assessment. She did, however, accept the offer of further contact with a social worker to review
her 'living conditions' in more detail. Arthur also agreed, although with
some apparent reluctance. The following day, the case was provisionally allocated to the social worker's student, who was in the second
year of a DipSW programme, having previously completed a successful
placement with a local authority assessment and care management
team. The current placement had been running for three months.

The progress of the case is taken up again presently. For the moment,
it is important to review the overall learning context in which the student was operating. The agency in question was the major provider of
placements to the student's DipSW programme, and had a general policy of placing students with practice teachers accredited on the basis of
holding (or currently being trained/assessed for) the Practice Teaching
Award. The practice teacher in question held the Award and worked

alongside a similarly qualified colleague, each taking a student every other year in rotation. The agency had been one of the first in the region to secure CCETSW approval in its own right as offering policies and facilities conducive to effective practice learning. Last but not least, the agency was a core partner in the joint provision of the DipSW programme itself.

This network, pioneering the comprehensive implementation of the CCETSW's composite strategy for promoting social work competence at qualifying level, has been outlined elsewhere (Slater, 1992). In the present context, a more detailed consideration is needed of the content and structure of the college-based teaching. In particular, the question needs to be posed: was elder abuse on the curriculum? Equally important, given Coulshed's strictures on 'curriculum overload', are structural questions relating to the magnitude and location of the subject in the curriculum, and the underlying rationale for its presence.

Adults 'pathway'

Very much in accordance with Coulshed's vision of curriculum integration, the DipSW programme in question requires all students to follow common modules provided under the organising rubrics of 'Social Work Theories and Methods', 'Social Problems and Social Policy', 'Social Work Law', 'Anti-discriminatory Practice' and, in the final year, 'Family Work'. At this level, the subject of elder abuse is inevitably broached, although specific inputs are necessarily diffuse in location and restricted in scope.

As the DipSW regulations themselves emphasise (CCETSW, 1995, p 19), 'deeper, more extensive understanding' relating to a specific service user group can only be promoted in tandem with similarly focused practice placements. This returns the discussion to 'areas of particular practice' or, in the most recent jargon, 'particular pathways'. The closed question of whether elder abuse is 'on the curriculum' in general terms now turns into the open question of what style of 'pathway' can most effectively promote integrated learning about elder abuse.

In the early 1990s the DipSW programme under consideration adopted a tripartite division into probation, children/families and adult areas of particular practice (Vass, 1996), thereby anticipating by several years the non-prescriptive example of particular pathways subsequently offered by the CCETSW (1995, p 13). A separate probation track had, of course, been a long-standing condition of Home Office funding, and the established status of children and families as a discrete area of work had recently been confirmed by the Children Act 1989. By contrast, the decision to mount a specific 'adults' pathway constituted an act of anti-oppressive defiance.

One has only to revisit the White Paper of 1989 to be reminded of the labelling that underpins community care policy. Unlike children's legislation, where a child is viewed first and foremost as such (ie as a child), adults in need of social support continue to be ascribed to atomistic categories ranging from 'illness and/or temporary disability', via 'old age, mental illness (including dementia), mental handicap, physical disability and sensory impairment', through to 'drug and alcohol related disorders, multiple handicaps and progressive illnesses such as AIDS or multiple sclerosis' (Department of Health, 1989, p 10).

Stealing a march on the Association of Metropolitan Authorities' (1995) call for radical reform of this chaotic and frequently offensive categorisation, the DipSW programme constructed a generic 'adults' pathway, subjecting such categories to critical examination. In particular, this entails a complex dialectic of genuinely physical conditions (eg an infection of the blood) and socially constructed limitations (eg age-based retirement from work irrespective of individual ability or motivation). The handiest formulation of this dialectic is probably in terms of an interplay between (individual) 'impairment' and (social) 'disabled-ness' (Crow, 1996).

The pernicious consequences of personalising what are essentially social processes are particularly well documented in relation to older adults. Indeed, the very act of constructing 'age' as a welfare category in the first place has been challenged as implying an intrinsic connection between later life and physical/mental decrepitude (Scrutton, 1990). The parallel obsession with 'protecting' older adults has been attacked as simultaneously effect and cause of this denigration (Iveson,

1990). More recently, the unconscious reproduction of ageist presuppositions on social work courses, including qualifying programmes, has been identified as a major barrier to effective learning about elder abuse in particular (Biggs et al, 1995).

Having surveyed the panoply of client categories (particularly 'age') in critical detail, the 'adults' pathway moves on to a consideration of community care policy. The continuing use of terms such as 'mental handicap' as recently as 1989 has already been commented on. At the same time, it is important to recognise that the White Paper plays down the significance of client labels in favour of a common focus on providing the services and support that people in these categories 'need to be able to live as independently as possible in their own homes' or in 'homely' substitute accommodation in the community (Department of Health, 1989, p 3).

The generic focus on individual 'need', as opposed to group identity, is reflected in a uniform process of professional intervention:

Care management and assessment constitute one integrated process for identifying and addressing the needs of individuals within available resources, recognising that those needs are unique to the individuals concerned. For this reason, care management and assessment emphasise adapting services to needs rather than fitting people into existing services, and dealing with the needs of the individual as a whole rather than assessing needs separately for different services. (Department of Health, 1991, p 9)

Inevitably, this model has been criticised for stopping short of handing direct control to users (Oliver, 1996). Nevertheless, numerous commentators subscribe to a differentiated assessment: the complex, contradictory components of current policy offer significant opportunities for 'mutation' in a progressive direction (Levick, 1992; Morris, 1993; Lewis and Glennerster, 1996). Of particular significance in the present context is the subsuming of older people in a generic 'adults' group. This provides a convenient bridge to elder abuse teaching, which, as one group of stakeholders has rightly warned, must not be allowed to foster an 'exclusive mystique and elitism about the subject' (Association of Directors of Social Services, 1995, p 15). The 'adults' pathway is insulated against these dangers by its very structure. In the first place, the subject is broached only after detailed study of community care arrangements, reflecting the official view that the latter is the appropriate context in which to frame elder abuse policies and guidelines (Department of Health, 1993), and endorsing the view of senior agency personnel that investigation of elder abuse should not be viewed as a wholly separate process (Department of Health, 1995).

Secondly, in accordance with the rationale of the entire pathway, elder abuse is presented within the broader context of 'adults at risk', paying particular attention to a pioneering document produced by the Association of Directors of Social Services (1991). The same generic concern is apparent in a later publication (Association of Directors of Social Services, 1995): although concerned with the 'mistreatment' of older people in particular, half of the text is devoted to the legal framework for intervention which, inevitably, is framed in terms of 'vulnerable adults' generally.

Proposals for reforming/extending the law reinforce such a focus on vulnerable adults. After five years of careful consideration, the Law Commission (1995) confirmed its original view that the particular problem of elder abuse should be tackled under the broader mantle of 'protection for vulnerable people at risk'. As a consequence, the concern to protect older people from abuse is immediately and explicitly tempered by respect for individual autonomy, including the right to take risks that might well seem unreasonable to others.

Conceived thus, teaching on elder abuse, far from fostering an 'exclusive mystique and elitism' (to recall the concern of the Association of Directors of Social Services), builds on and consolidates the underlying concern with adulthood that constitutes the starting point of the pathway as a whole. This was dramatically confirmed by a classroom-based presentation of the case of 'Lucie Ziegler', which is now concluded.

Conclusion of case study

The initial details of the case have already revealed that, although the original referral from the police via the GP had been conceived in terms of a need for psychiatric attention, the client had been hostile to this formulation and had agreed only to further intervention in the form of a general consideration of her 'living conditions'. The vagueness of this phrase proved particularly helpful, setting the scene for a joint exploration of how Lucie lived, how she wanted to live and what options were available. Such a perspective could legitimately encompass a full range of factors from washing and dressing to protection from serious injury.

In the first instance, social work intervention meant forming a working relationship with Lucie, valuing her as someone who existed within social networks, who shared responsibility for her fate and who was capable of making informed choices. A cynical observer might well have questioned the relevance of such an approach to an elderly woman whose uneven communication skills had been interpreted as 'confusion' by more than one party. In the event, such reservations merely serve to make the outcome of the intervention all the more striking: in the course of only three individual contacts, Lucie's alertness, interest and communication skills had improved to the point where she began, with help, to undertake an extensive review of her circumstances, options and wishes.

At one level, the assessment concentrated on Lucie's need for help with washing and dressing, in the light of her obvious state of physical neglect. Inevitably, this involved an exploration of her personal standards and current sense of self-worth. It soon emerged that such resources were overshadowed by Lucie's sense of being 'at the mercy' of Arthur. Responding to patient and attentive listening, she not only repeated the substance of the allegations previously made to the police but did so in a manner remarkable for its confidence and lucidity. This entailed extensive and fully coherent detail of financial comings and goings, together with dramatic and chronological accounts of being forced into unwanted sex, including an allegation of drunken rape on the previous Christmas Eve.

In response to gentle probing, Lucie gave an equally lucid account of what for her had been a painful and humiliating 'interrogation' by two male police officers. The student explained that future contacts with the police and judiciary could be eased by support from a friend or advocate. But Lucie was (and subsequently remained) adamant about one thing: she did not intend to subject herself to further 'ordeals' with 'the law'. At the same time, she was (and also remained) equally clear as to what she did want: help to assert her financial and physical independence of Arthur, while remaining for the time being under the same roof, sharing each other's company on an equal footing.

Obviously, the allegation of abuse demanded an urgent review of the case's allocation to a student. Fortunately, the agency had a clear policy in this regard, first formulated in the submission for CCETSW approval (London Borough of Enfield, 1990) and subsequently included in a user-friendly practice learning brochure:

> While the agency's duty of care precludes the direct allocation to students of cases involving serious risk to clients or others, practice teachers are actively encouraged to draw on such work for practice learning purposes via a range of shadowing, co-working and sub-contracting arrangements. (London Borough of Enfield, 1996, p 6)

In accordance with this principle, it was agreed that practice teacher and student would co-work the case for the foreseeable future, reviewing the feasibility of this arrangement in weekly supervision sessions. Thus, while client safety would remain the paramount consideration, the case's potential as a vehicle for social work learning would be capitalised on to the full.

Unlike a police investigation, subsequent contact with the alleged perpetrator was not aimed at establishing evidence or otherwise of crime and guilt, but at confronting Arthur with Lucie's allegations and inviting him to consider his own position in the emerging scenario. His explanation of the specifically financial allegations was along the lines of normal relations between a cohabiting couple, where boundaries of ownership become blurred on both sides. Allegations of rape, by contrast, were dismissed as not merely untrue but malicious. He described the allegations as particularly hurtful, given his genuine affection for Lucie. At the same time, he complained of the increasingly onerous responsibility of caring for her, and expressed doubts as to how long he could 'go on'.

Taken in conjunction with Lucie's desire to re-establish her autonomy, and in particular to reduce her dependence on Arthur, the latter's acknowledgement of caring difficulties opened up considerable possibilities for 'systemic' family work. While acknowledging the seriousness of Lucie's allegations against Arthur, it was vital that social work personnel should disavow the role of judge and jury. Equally, without prejudice to the possible consequences of future allegations, it was important to move beyond the language of crime and punishment to a new 'script' (Baldock and Ungerson, 1994) of mutual user and carer need, mediated by appropriate community care services. The strategic objective for any such intervention was unanimously agreed as the need to guarantee Lucie's physical and emotional security, while simultaneously reducing the caring pressures on Arthur.

Social work intervention had succeeded in opening up a previously closed system, a transformation graphically reflected in Lucie's growing attention to her physical appearance. To consolidate this shift, while avoiding long-term dependence on social work staff, the next task was to complete an assessment report in accordance with local care management procedures so as to secure the funding of appropriate services. Fortunately, the assessment, although undertaken from a hospital base, had already been conceived in the language of 'user and carer need'. Somewhat more problematic was the establishment of 'eligibility', which required the complex commensuration of 'physical disability' factors with related, but logically distinct, indicators of 'risk of significant harm'.

Above all, the agreement of a care plan at a multi-disciplinary case conference centred on a shared understanding of the strategic role of home care in sustaining and monitoring the reconstructed living unit. The case conference also offered an opportunity to confer with representatives of the local domestic violence unit on a more effective police response to possible future calls from Lucie or people in similar circumstances. Last but not least, the specifically practice-based lessons of this particular case could be considered more generally under the auspices of an ongoing review of the lead agency's 'Abuse of Vulnerable Adults' policy, which had already achieved a national profile (Pritchard, 1995, appendix 2).

Following the case conference, the student's placement schedule left sufficient time for her to introduce the home care worker to Lucie and Arthur, and to monitor the change process for several weeks. Over this period, Lucie's physical appearance and overall demeanour continued to improve. Additionally, she gradually resumed control of her own finances, including visits to the post office to cash her giro, with the assistance of the home care worker. Above all, Lucie confirmed that she was enjoying a life free of the threat of violence. Arthur too acknowledged that things had changed for the better in the sense of 'quietening down a bit'.

Practical conclusions

On reflection, it is apparent that the case holds enormous potential for promoting professional understanding about elder abuse. Indeed, a Ziegler/Wilson case study has already been developed for use in a variety of staff development and academic initiatives, although this necessarily entails considerable condensation of detail and complexity, particularly as regards the role of the police.

The present chapter, by contrast, is concerned specifically with social work learning at qualifying level, and this has entailed extensive coverage of the case work, together with an exhaustive account of the overall learning network, comprising an accredited practice teacher, an approved practice learning agency and an associated DipSW programme offering a discrete 'adults' pathway. In particular, the chapter has described a situation in which direct practice-learning opportunities involving elder abuse were made available to a final year student on this pathway without compromising the agency's paramount duty of care to clients.

In concluding, it is important to highlight the major practical lessons of the Ziegler/Wilson case. These must not be confused with an individualised record of the actual learning achieved by the student concerned, which is a matter for the DipSW programme's assessment panel. Rather, the present task is to distil the case's inherent learning potential or, to use current educational jargon, its 'indicative learning outcomes'. Reflecting social work's long-standing concern with the integration of theory and practice, each of the following points is accompanied by a reference to relevant reading:

- Presenting needs, even as articulated by professionals, may mask other and more serious problems (Department of Health, 1991).
- Counselling can help older people to review their lives and tackle major problems (O'Leary, 1996).
- Elder abuse blights lives (Eastman, 1984).
- Professional responses to elder abuse should be guided (not regimented) by practice guidelines (Penhale, 1993).
- Social problems are the malfunctioning of a network of people (Smale et al, 1994).
- Professional instincts to protect people from harm must be tempered by respect for adult autonomy (Law Commission, 1995).
- Abusive relationships may be transcribed into the language of community care need/eligibility (Department of Health, 1995).
- Interpersonal skills are essential to effective assessment of need (Sheppard, 1995).
- Victims of elder abuse should participate appropriately in setting objectives for individual care plans (Department of Health, 1993).
- Care plans should specify how risk is to be managed (Hargreaves and Hughes, 1996).
- Introduction of services requires careful attention and sensitive handling (Smale et al, 1993).
- Care services, even of modest scope, can exert a profound beneficial/preventative effect on family systems (Clark et al, 1998).
- Social work with older people can help raise their morale and reduce vulnerability (Sinclair et al, 1990).

Readers will have noticed that over half of these points, together with the titles of the relevant reading, are not formulated with specific reference to elder abuse as such. Instead, they focus variously on adults at risk, assessment and care management processes, systems theory in general and principles of social work practice with older adults in particular.

This confirms that elder abuse can be 'on the curriculum' (to recall Kingston et al's question) without compounding Coulshed's nightmare scenario of 'a dash of this and a drop of that'. On the contrary, far from contributing to curriculum overload, specific teaching on elder abuse can be mounted under Coulshed's 'organising rubrics' in such a way as to actively promote curriculum integration.

Acknowledgement

The authors acknowledge with thanks the assistance of Richard Walton, social worker and practice teacher, in preparing this chapter.

Elder abuse in care and nursing settings: detection and prevention

Les Bright

The author of the most extensive research review in the field of elder abuse had the following to say about care and nursing settings:

> Little is known about abuse in communal settings. It appears that psychological abuse is the most common form of abuse and relates to many of the pressures of looking after people with severe disabilities. The need for work-based training is clearly demonstrated. The provisions for registration and inspection of homes offer a front line approach to the prevention of abuse but their effectiveness depends on the allocation of sufficient resources. (McCreadie, 1996, p vi)

Those few lines drawn from Claudine McCreadie's research update capture the problem, provide a signpost to the issues to be considered, highlight the importance of a trained workforce, and identify the strength and weakness of inspectoral activity. They provide an agenda for policy makers, operational managers and their staff groups and for the author of the present chapter.

'Little is known'

Why is so little known, or why are we prepared to accept that statement as accurate if we *do* know more? Are residential and nursing homes all located out of view and of little importance to the wider community? The Registered Homes Act 1984 has been in effect for more than ten years, and the requirement on registration authorities to publish reports of their annual inspections of residential care homes has been in place since a Department of Health direction to them in 1994 (LAC(94)16). After sustained pressure from a number of quarters, the government issued instructions to health authorities, in late 1997, requiring them to adopt a system of 'open reporting' for their inspections of nursing homes, with effect from April 1998. This action, which was long overdue, went some way towards lifting the veil of secrecy surrounding such institutions.

Both the growth of advocacy and the emergence of a specialist voluntary organisation to support relatives of people in care homes have contributed to a climate in which greater attention has been paid to the kind of life that residents can expect if they decide to move to a care home. The promotion of consumerism, via charters, complaints systems and lay involvement in inspection, has also been responsible for service users apparently having more power than in former times. Yet, it is still possible to say, 'little is known ...'

Whenever newspaper or broadcast journalists shine their lights into this corner of society they seem to have very little difficulty in finding current or former staff prepared to talk about their experiences. Relatives also come forward with stories that they had felt unable to tell, for fear of the impact on their loved ones while they were alive or to protect themselves from further distress at a time of bereavement (Alzheimer's Disease Society, 1997; Bright, 1997). In the same year two broadsheet newspapers launched campaigns focused on standards of care for older people in care homes and hospital settings; the former was addressed in *The Sunday Times* in a series entitled 'Who Cares?' (from 31 August) and the latter in the *Observer* through a parallel series headed 'Dignity on the Ward' (from 5 October). To these can be added radio and television programmes responding to the news and political agenda or perceived public interest, exposing sharp practices and abusive behaviour.

The professional press also picks up concerns from time to time, resulting in the appearance of isolated articles or features comprising groups of articles. An article in the *Nursing Times* (Inman and Sone, 1997), for example, explored the growing influence of American health-care companies in the UK market and recounted the stories of a number of qualified staff who had experienced very worrying trends in the care regimes they had been asked to operate. If we add this lengthy list of sources of information to the regular items in the columns of both *Community Care* and *Nursing Times* – telling of suspensions, sackings and court appearances for mistreatment, assault and theft – and to reports of scandals uncovered with depressing regularity over the past 30 years, the question must become, 'Why, if we have known so much for so long, do we still tell ourselves that little is known?'

It might be suggested that we know enough – or even too much – to allow us to take steps to turn the situation round, but that we are daunted by the task and feel powerless. There are more than 20,000 premises registered to give care to people in need, of which the vast majority cater for older people, and more than 500,000 people work in care homes. The workforce is very varied, with only a minority trained and qualified in appropriate disciplines, and, as ever, the cost implications of bringing about change cast a shadow of pessimism.

Types of abuse

Writers and researchers have identified five main types of abuse (physical, psychological, sexual, financial and neglect), though these may not represent the fullness of the experience of residents of care homes. They may be the victims of racial abuse and of spiritual abuse – distinctly different from psychological abuse, touching as they do on personal identity and self-worth, and long-held and deeply felt beliefs about the world and one's place in it. Lengthening the typology does nothing, however, to illuminate what is meant by abuse so that it can be better understood and so that programmes of training, induction and orientation may be established to affect the performance of staff working with vulnerable people. Producing definitions, while useful to those whose work involves them in writing policies and procedures, may have the effect of disguising the routine indignity that many people may be exposed to day by day, throughout the day and possibly night time too.

Many people find the very idea of sexual abuse of older people not just repugnant but unbelievable. Thankfully, the incidence of sexual abuse and assault is not reckoned to be high, though perhaps the tag 'little is known' may be particularly resonant in this instance. Sexual abuse is a prominent feature of the abuse of other dependent groups of people (Craft, 1996), and is at the centre of the deliberations of the tribunal investigating abuse in children's homes in North Wales. One of the most highly publicised cases of effective 'whistle-blowing' in the care sector is concerned with how the deputy matron of a privately run nursing home took steps that led to the arrest, and subsequently the conviction, of the home's owner for serious sexual assaults on three frail, dependent and very elderly women (Public Concern at Work, 1997).

Physical assaults are not generally seen as a widespread problem. However, this view is open to challenge, partly because of differing perceptions of the word 'assault' and also because of concern about the level of under-reporting by staff of the ways in which their colleagues may carry out their duties.

'Rough handling' is a term that seems to have a meaning only with those engaged in looking after other people. It is a 'professional' term describing an unprofessional act – using undue force, and applying it inappropriately – that would be viewed by the wider public as bullying, threatening or cruel. Financial abuse, or theft as it might be better described, also takes place. Sometimes it is discovered and action is taken; sometimes it is discovered and no action is taken; and on other occasions it occurs but goes unrecognised, or receives de facto endorsement by appalling ageist attitudes such as, 'she doesn't need any money' or 'he doesn't miss it, and wouldn't know what to with it'. Wealthier residents may be at risk of fraud, theft or pressure to 'give away' cash and other assets. The most financially impoverished, reliant on Income Support to provide them with a weekly personal expenses allowance amounting to about 30 per cent of the sum that independent commentators have determined as adequate (Parker, 1996), may be using this money to top up an equally inadequate sum available to pay their fees. There is anecdotal evidence in confidential exchanges of correspondence from residents or their relatives/advocates that some providers see this allowance as being available to them and design contracts that bind the resident to pay £10.00, from the £14.45 personal allowance (1998 figures), towards their care costs. Other residents' relatives may view this allowance as an addition to their weekly income – a kind of 'back payment' for care services they provided without pay for the years before admission to a care home.

Neglect is in some ways as shocking as sexual or physical assault in that people seek the refuge of life in a home as a result of being unable to look after themselves satisfactorily (Department of Health, 1994a). That failing physical or mental health should be compounded by professional neglect is a slur on all those working in this field and leads to public mistrust, which in turn does nothing to build the confidence of new residents or their families at a time when they may be anxious about the decision they feel has been forced on them by circumstances. Being left in a urine-soaked bed, deliberately under-fed or under-stimulated, or kept in a room that is too cold can be explained in a number of ways, with the common factor of keeping down unit costs sitting in the centre presiding over a workforce that may be under-trained, under-valued and certainly under-paid. This provides us with an explanation why people paid to care for others fail, but it can in no way provide a justification for such behaviour.

Psychological abuse has long been associated with the stresses of caring for dependent older people (Eastman, 1984, 1994). With the current policy of maintaining people in their own homes as long as is feasible, elderly residents of care homes are likely to have increased levels of dependency (Nolan, 1996). As a result, many of them will need to be toileted during the night, to be turned every couple of hours and to have the bed changed as a result of incontinence and the shortcomings of pads. Other residents will need help with eating and drinking, and constant reassurance because they may feel lonely and afraid during daylight hours as well as at night. Such power over the lives of people provides scope for abusive actions, as many of the activities described above are performed in private and one-to-one between care giver and cared for. Hurtful words can be exchanged without anybody else being aware, voice tone can convey threats that could not be uttered in the presence of others, and the dependent person can feel belittled and humiliated as a result of the way in which their need is described, in their presence, to a third party – either another carer or another resident. Raised voices, harsh words or no words are undoubtedly much too widespread and accepted by residents as the price they must pay for being looked after.

Views from the field

Talking with managers and staff about the things that bother them in the way that residents are cared for, I have uncovered a wide seam of poor practice that I have described as a 'dripping tap' of daily indignities. I asked them to tell me what they meant by abuse, not simply to recite the 30-word definition adopted by Action on Elder Abuse, or the five types that the textbooks and journal articles tell them constitute abuse. Initial uneasiness soon gives way to a wide ranging and ultimately chilling list of actions that may have taken hold of their own or colleagues' work. There are predictable topics such as restricting choices, invading privacy and making fun of residents – with matching excuses, frequently centred on the idea of doing the best for people unable to make decisions for themselves. It has also been possible to uncover other practices that might not be considered harmful but which doubtless cause alarm for anyone engaged in residential care. How is it possible to explain 'listening to residents' conversations in their rooms, using the intercom, as a form of staff entertainment', as one workshop participant reported, in any other way than as abuse? Taken alongside reports that residents are being fed their breakfast while sitting on a commode, in front of another resident and staff, we are able to find clear examples of homes that devise routines that attend to the needs of the staff working in them, and address residents' needs only tangentially or as an afterthought (Bright, 1997; Jenkins, 1997).

Jenkins (1997) describes the process she went through in order to transform a home with neglected patients and anxious, hostile staff into a haven. When she took the job of matron, the home for which she was to be responsible was referred to as a hell-hole. Jenkins was able to substantiate this claim when she trailed round behind the night care team whom she had instructed to follow their usual routine. Patients 'were hauled out of bed and plonked on commodes' in their wet night-clothes. 'Throned in indignity, this was where they had breakfast' (p 27). This was occurring in a nursing home at 5.00am!

An analysis

With views from nearly 1,800 owners, managers and care staff from both residential and nursing homes over a two-year period, it is possible to identify common themes. It is then more possible to focus effectively on the actions that can be taken by various stakeholders.

- *Routines* We do it this way, we have always done it this way, I don't give it any thought. (Denies choices to residents: about meals, bedtimes etc.)
- *Regimes* This is the way in which this institution functions, it's right, and unchangeable. (Demands that residents comply with norms, conspires against good individualised care practices.)
- *Rules* This is what I have been told to do, I am not allowed to do things differently. (Binds the carer to ways of doing things that treat residents as people who have things done to them, not as people in need of assistance.)
- *Repetition* Performing the same task many times each shift, many times for each resident. (Leads to carelessness, or lack of attention to detail.)
- *Resentment* Low pay, low skill base, low personal and professional esteem. (Causes staff to perform less well, perhaps to see people they are looking after as the reason for their predicament – occupying a low-pay job.)

A major weakness of this approach has to be acknowledged: it focuses on poor practice, rather than rooting out some of the extreme and unlawful behaviour that comes before the courts. However, it is worth noting that hidden away in this wide variety of responses from practitioners and managers are statements as stark and frightening as hitting, poking, pushing, pinching and slapping as well as tormenting and ridiculing. In being prepared to suggest that such actions occur in their own workplace, or another with which they are familiar, they are asking for strategies to combat them.

How can we respond?

The need for a more highly trained workforce is widely accepted, though the tools and conditions to deliver this may not be as freely available as is necessary or desirable. The development of National Vocational Qualifications (or Scottish Vocational Qualifications) has provided opportunities for many more staff, and is having a positive effect on the skill level and mix in care homes. But the development is uneven: it is possible to visit homes where all staff have been through, or are undergoing, this important experience of assessed work and planned assignments – often judged by peers whom they trust and respect – but it is depressingly just as easy to find homes in which such training takes a rather obvious back seat.

Commissioning service provision

The shift in ownership from the public sector, with an infrastructure to support training activity, to a market place where the private sector is now pre-eminent creates new challenges for those organising training. Although there has been some turbulence as mergers, take-overs and counter-take-overs have occurred among some of the larger corporate interests, the reality is that most homes remain in the hands of small enterprises, frequently sole traders or husband and wife teams, operating just one home. Their capacity to release staff for training may be severely affected both by the scale of their operation and by the financial implications at a time when it may reasonably be claimed that homes fees have not been growing at the same rate as their costs. If the business is existing on very narrow margins, it is tempting not to invest any scarce resources – be they staff or cash – in something that has no immediate pay-off. Those who make decisions about the placement of older people in need of residential care should think about how they can use the contracting process to bring in higher standards. A sliding scale of fees reflecting support for homes where there is a clear commitment to training across the whole staff team, enhanced as more candidates succeed in achieving their stated goals, could have an immediate effect on the intentions of those who do not presently give priority to spending in that direction. Commissioners of services have the power to specify in this way and some already do. The contracting process is not a substitute for inspection activity but a complement to it, providing detailed specifications to back up overall requirements. Moving on from 'appropriately qualified staff' to identifying particular training experiences necessary to satisfy purchasers (eg 'all staff shall have attended a course enabling them to detect abuse, and take appropriate action to protect residents') addresses the need for staff to reflect on whether they are unnecessarily bound by routines or have developed resentment towards the very people they are expected to be looking after.

Setting standards

Standards are applicable not just to care homes but also to the people who work in them. Discussion of the need to spread the opportunities for training must also take account of ways of controlling the employment of individuals, including ways of barring those whose performance is unacceptable from taking up similar employment elsewhere. The Professional Conduct Committee of the United Kingdom Central Council for Nursing, Midwifery and Health Visiting (UKCC) has the power to strike off a nurse whose work is poor and on whom they receive adverse reports from their employer, so they may not be able to take up another nursing post. No such system exists for people who are unqualified or who seek out posts for which a nursing qualification is not required. Proposals to establish a General Social Care Council, and government acceptance of its importance, are very welcome and will create ways to regulate the performance of all practitioners, regardless of the functions they perform. Again, commissioners of services should be able to specify, as a condition of making a contract, that staff are registered.

Valuing care services

If we accept that one of the reasons why care staff may perform badly is associated with the resentment they feel about occupying a low-status, low-pay job in a corner of society that seems to have a light shone on it only for the purpose of condemning it, a major task confronts us. Encouraging the general public to see residential care and nursing home activity as being as important as the work that nurses undertake in hospitals is a modest goal. Convincing opinion formers, and public opinion, to translate that into a commitment to spending more money, so that the call for higher standards can be backed up by the money to pay for it, is significantly more ambitious but also must remain a goal, albeit with a longer time-scale than other parts of the prescription written here.

Inspection

Inspection is judged harshly from many quarters. Providers claim that inspectors are unrealistic in their expectations and overly pernickety, while the relatively new breed of social services staff – contracts managers and commissioners – see it as being focused far too much on the tangibles such as the fabric of the building and numbers of staff employed, to the exclusion of quality of care issues. Yet another group of people, among them relatives of residents and advocacy organisations, consider it to be another bit of bureaucracy. On the other hand, inspections themselves can fall victim to insufficient resources. The statutory annual report of the chief executive of one of Britain's largest cities, on the work of the authority's inspection unit, carried news that three-quarters of the city's homes had not been inspected in the previous year (Valios, 1997). This highlights how critical it is for such units to be adequately staffed, if even relatively modest statutory requirements are to be fulfilled.

Given that many of the patterns of abusive behaviour described to me have occurred in the privacy of a resident's own room, and are therefore not routinely witnessed by other members of staff, it is just as unrealistic to expect inspectors to pick up such events either in the context of their annual inspection visit or during one of the unannounced visits the legislation permits them to make. Inspectors do observe staff, do talk to residents (and are helped in this now by lay assessors accompanying them on their visits) and do pick up problems and weaknesses in staff performance and behaviour. There is some disagreement as to whether inspectors should merely record these and expect the manager to take action, or if they themselves should more pro-actively set out to change staff attitudes and performance. The credibility and reputation of inspection would be enhanced if it were encouraged and funded to move beyond defining problems into demonstrating what action should be taken to rectify faults. Leading by example will be expensive, and not always the most appropriate way of dealing with an identified problem. Continuing resource constraints may mean that there is a case to be made for a narrower, less interventionist approach where inspection focuses on ensuring that providers have adopted, and are following, policies and procedures that will have the effect of assuring the quality of service available to residents.

Policies and procedures

Inspectors can play a key part in ensuring that homes create environments in which it is less easy for abusive behaviour to take root and flourish. The following four linked activities can be specified and subsequently monitored:

- policies stating what the home intends to do, and why, providing a safe and secure place in which to live where the key values for a good life are upheld (Department of Health, 1989a);
- procedures outlining the way this will be done, outlining the respective roles of management and staff;
- guidelines assisting staff at all levels, giving information on types of abuse, and common indicators;
- training to assist in implementation.

Such policies as are adopted ought to be a product of collaborative activity in the home, involving all staff, and should be the subject of consultation with residents and their relatives. Obviously, great sensitivity will be necessary in order to avoid creating distress and alarm. The inspection process can act as part of an annual review of the policy and its effectiveness, ensuring that it adapts to changes in circumstances, and to personnel too.

Clusters of concern

The process of designing and then implementing this framework should have the effect of bringing to the surface other more general concerns about the way in which the home operates. These concerns are likely to be fairly reliable indicators of the scope for abuse to occur or for the home to be something like a 'failing school', to use the terminology of education and the Office for Standards in Education.

If a home is poorly managed, with staff receiving inadequate training and poor supervision, problems of morale and low self-esteem are likely to be evident. Poor staff management can take many forms, including rotas being badly arranged, with too few staff perhaps leading to insufficient time and inadequate systems to effect a meaningful handover from one shift to another. Problems in recruiting or retaining staff, leading to excessive use of agency personnel, or to a small staff group working excessively long hours will lead to tiredness and to more erratic behaviour. Ultimately, residents pay a high price for such routine and avoidable shortcomings.

Giving attention to the general management of the home, to ensure that employees are carefully selected, fully inducted, regularly supervised and sympathetically supported, is the single most important step to be taken to prevent abuse. Being clear about the tasks to be undertaken by staff, so that a clear and detailed job description and person specification can be produced and then used for the advertising and appointment process, is equally important in ensuring that the right people join the team. They should then be inculcated with the values and ethos of a home that rewards staff with good conditions of service

– not just monetary (often the most difficult to deliver) – where they can feel positive about the people they are looking after, and nurtured as an asset to the business.

Conclusion

I have argued that, despite the absence of research, plenty is known about abuse in care homes. Although it is possible neither to quantify this nor to produce evidence of prevalence, it is possible to describe the forms it takes and to provide explanations for its occurrence.

To prevent or detect abuse by staff it is necessary to have established policies and procedures that define both the purposes of the home and the parts that those who work there will play in fulfilling those objectives. Offering training to staff and involving them and the residents in the design and implementation of any policies and procedures are likely to add to their effectiveness, and to spread ownership and responsibility for performance and subsequent reviews of performance.

The White Paper that led to the National Health Service and Community Care Act 1990 described the changes to be brought about by the Act as aiming to 'enable people to live as normal a life as possible in their own homes or in a homely environment in the local community' and to 'give people a greater individual say in how they live their lives and the services they need to help them to do so' (Department of Health, 1989b, p 4). Requiring all registered homes to adopt policies and procedures for the prevention and detection of abuse is entirely consistent with the Act, and with the reasonable hopes people ought to have for a happy old age.

Learning from others: elder abuse in international perspective

Britt-Inger Saveman

Although researchers and practitioners have tried, during the last 20 years, to highlight elder abuse as a new phenomenon, cultural writings such as Greek myths, biblical passages, legends, fairy tales and novels, as well as history, all reveal elder abuse (Reinharz, 1986). Violence against parents was regarded as a criminal act in Sweden from 1600 to 1850, when the Old Testament commandment about honouring your parents was applied in the Swedish courts of justice. Between 1750 and 1850 more than half the cases of violence in the criminal statistics available in Sweden concerned violence against parents, which could lead to capital punishment. In the middle of the nineteenth century the registration of violence against parents was abolished, decriminalising abuse of the elderly and effectively making it invisible (Odén, 1991, 1994).

Much has been done about elder abuse since the first reports came from the USA in the late 1970s (Block and Sinnott, 1979; Lau and Kosberg, 1979), but this does not mean that we can relax and think that we have all the knowledge needed. Research studies vary in their design and approach, and so do the results. Cultural and social as well as medical contexts also vary between countries, which makes it hard to compare results. Much of the complexity in elder abuse cases is context dependent. Thus, more comparative research is of the utmost importance. Many literature reviews have been made, an excellent example being that by McCreadie (1996) covering almost all that is known from research. The focus concerning elder abuse has turned increasingly towards elder abuse in institutions and residential care, although few research data have been published about elder abuse in an institutional context.

Many of the professionals who see elder abuse experience strong feelings, such as powerlessness, anger and despair. These professionals from several countries report that there is a lack of knowledge of how to deal with elder abuse. It is clear, however, that wherever elder abuse occurs it leads to suffering for the abused person and to problems for anyone witnessing it, for the rest of the family and for the staff who have to deal with it.

The aim of this chapter is to review some international studies of elder abuse, focusing on the European, and especially the Scandinavian, studies, and to discuss their implications for practice.

Elder abuse in Europe

When looking at the research results and knowledge available about elder abuse in European countries, it seems that research and implementation studies reported in the English language come predominantly from the UK and Scandinavia. However, this perception might not be accurate because there is a language barrier between the countries in Europe. A brief review is gained from two journals, *Social Work in Europe* and the *Journal of Elder Abuse & Neglect*, both of which had special issues in 1995 concerning elder abuse in international, European and cross-cultural perspectives. The situation in, for example, Italy, Spain, the Netherlands, Norway, France, Poland, Greece and Ireland was highlighted.

The report from Ireland deals with how elder abuse is framed as a social problem as well as with the importance of inter-agency co-ordination similar to that for child abuse cases. One research study was based on 14 elder abuse cases identified at a hospital department of geriatric medicine (O'Loughlin, 1995), and reports from voluntary organisations confirm the existence of elder abuse. However, no official data have been gathered, and little government concern has been directed to the problem (Horkan, 1995).

In France, Italy, Greece, Poland and Spain the family structure and the change it is undergoing, together with demographic changes, are highlighted as factors essential to an understanding of elder abuse and its causes. These might explain why elder abuse is more or less invisible and needs to be examined more closely (Halicka, 1995; Ochotorena and Larrión Zugasti, 1995; Ogg, 1995; Pitsiou-Darrough and Spinellis, 1995; Ripamonti, 1995). From Poland it is reported that, with the exception of isolated instances, elder abuse has not yet been identified and its existence only marginally suggested. However, it is suggested that psychological abuse occurs more often in the family, whereas physical abuse is more common outside the family (Halicka, 1995). In Greece a research study involving 750 older people found that the major forms of abuse were verbal and physical. A rate of 154 mistreated elders per 1,000 older citizens was reported, half this number being abused by a family member. It is possible that certain types of abuse are not so defined because they are acceptable to some extent in Greek society (Pitsiou-Darrough and Spinellis, 1995).

Although bearing the language barrier in mind, there seems to be a lack of research results and intervention strategies reported from France (cf Ogg, 1995) and Italy. However, the Women against Violence Centre in Italy has reported a large number of older women being abused in their own homes (Ripamonti, 1995). In Spain a few research studies have been carried out, but are all published in Spanish. During 1996/97 Spain was one of three countries that worked in an EU-funded project concerning elder abuse in residential care (reported later in this chapter).

A research group composed of members from Norway, Finland and Sweden worked together for several years in the early 1990s, in order to improve knowledge from an interdisciplinary point of view. The researchers were drawn from the disciplines of history, nursing, sociology, social work, medicine and social anthropology. In their work they struggled with three basic problems:

- the difficulties of establishing a definition of the phenomenon of abuse;
- the lack of national funding to carry out their research;
- the distrust of colleagues, government officials and policy makers owing to the 'invisibility' of the problem of abuse of the elderly (Hydle, 1993, 1994).

There has been some change in attitude in recent years. Funding has been given to elder abuse research (eg the ongoing study in Sweden about violence in residential care), and official reports of mistreatment have been produced from, for example, the National Board of Health and Welfare in Sweden (1994, 1995).

Elder abuse – what does it mean?

One way of coming closer to the phenomenon is to agree what we include and exclude when we talk about elder abuse, not only in research but also in practice. In almost every written document about the subject there is a discussion of elder abuse, maltreatment and mistreatment, and what these constitute. Its content and related attributes, such as age and dependency, as well as its typology seem to be never-ending topics of discussion. This ongoing discussion has, of course, an impact on both research and practice. For more details concerning definitions/descriptions, see for example McCreadie (1996) and Saveman (1994). In this chapter I highlight two suggested definitions – one with an analytical emphasis (Johns et al, 1991) and one concerning elder abuse in residential care (Eastman et al, 1997).

Norwegian researchers have focused on the problem of defining abuse of the elderly, applying a social anthropological perspective. They suggest that abuse should be seen in its social context and that it has to be judged by a third party, the witness (Johns et al, 1991). Their analytical definition has an all-embracing meaning:

> Abuse is a social act with at least two actors, where the one actor violates the personal boundaries of the other. This act is abuse if interpreted and valued as illegitimate by a third person, the witness. (Hydle and Johns, 1992, p 58)

The Norwegian definition is in line with how district nurses in one of the Swedish studies reported their attempts to describe elder abuse (Saveman et al, 1993a). They did not use a distinct definition but described abuse of older people as 'overstepping the boundaries of a person's autonomy/integrity' and they gave examples from specific situations, adopting a line of reasoning that seemed to guide them in identifying abuse. They put themselves in the abused people's shoes in order to understand their experience. How to judge the case as abusive or not seemed to be very difficult.

A definition or description of elder abuse/mistreatment must be made available to all care staff and others who need to be able to detect mistreatment. Whatever definition one prefers or finds most useful, it should be tested and used in practice to ensure that it captures what we all mean when we talk about elder abuse in a family context or in institutional and residential settings. The definition might be a help to staff, as there is a risk that people see elder abuse only from their own perspective and this can lead to discrepancies between them. For example, a medical perspective – in which diagnosis is generally made from objective data – might have problems seeing the moral and subjective aspects of elder abuse. In the medical arena, most often objective data form the basis for diagnosing. Problems in identifying and defining abuse are described in research studies, and some general descriptions have been sought (Saveman et al, 1993a).

The lack of a clear definition may explain why staff are unsure whether an act in residential care might be abusive and whether they should report it. Restrictions on residents' movements and actions comprise one such example that would be considered by some people to constitute mistreatment but by others as acceptable or even necessary in certain circumstances. The European group that worked with pan-European preventive strategies and recommendations in an EU-funded project suggested the following definition of elder abuse in residential care:

> Elder abuse/mistreatment in a residential setting means any action or negligence on the part of staff, relatives or relevant others which constitutes inappropriate treatment or which violates the rights of residents and to which the resident objects or could reasonably be expected to object. (Eastman et al, 1997, p 7)

This definition, in contrast to that from Norway, presumes that the elderly persons themselves or their advocates are best suited to judge the situation as abusive and to object to it. Nevertheless, it is important to be able to discuss in as wide a forum as possible how to define and diagnose elder abuse.

Elder abuse – what does it look like?

In spite of all research efforts, our knowledge of the prevalence of older people being abused is poor. It is estimated that about 4 per cent of the older population (excluding mentally impaired older people) are victims of abuse (Pillemer and Finkelhor, 1988; Podnieks, 1992). In Finland an epidemiological study including 1,086 older people living in a semi-industrialised town indicated that 5 per cent had been abused in their homes. Psychological and financial abuse were most commonly reported. The conditions of the abused persons were characterised by poor health, loneliness and poor family relations (Kivelä et al, 1992). Qualitative studies of families receiving help from the Finnish First Homes Federation revealed that alcohol abuse seems to be more closely related to patterns of family violence in Finland than in the other Nordic countries (Kivelä, 1994).

In Sweden 8 per cent of a random sample of 934 Swedish adults knew of older people being abused (in most cases financially) during one year. Of these, 26 per cent reported a family member as the abuser and 20 per cent reported a professional carer (Tornstam, 1989). In a similar study from Denmark the overall incidence was almost the same but with few reports of staff as the abusers (Tornstam, 1989).

In another Swedish study, 6 per cent of 474 close family members caring for a relative with dementia spontaneously admitted to psychological and physical abuse. In mitigation they mentioned their own poor health and limited social contacts (Grafström et al, 1993a). In a follow-up study two years later, none of them owned up to abusive behaviour (Grafström et al, 1993b).

Forty-four instances of elder abuse related by district nurses in Sweden revealed that the cases were complex, and that they often concerned families providing care for an older person. The carer as well as the person cared for could be the one abused, or the abuse could be mutual. The acts of abuse and the relationships between the parties, as well as the characters of the abused and the abuser, were in line with findings in other studies. The main finding from the perspective of the district nurses was that the abuse seemed to be related to the inability of one party to meet the care demands required by the elderly person, by the carer or by the specific situation. It also seemed to be related to a history of violence. These situations were characterised by lack of love, an inhibiting dependence between the parties and the negative execution of power by the stronger over the weaker party (Saveman et al, 1996).

Formal reports were used in three Swedish studies. In the first study, 12 per cent of the district nurses in one county council reported 30 cases of elder abuse during a six-month period (Saveman et al, 1993b). In the second, home care staff from four parts of Sweden reported 97 cases of abuse during the previous two years (Saveman and Norberg, 1993) and, in the third study, district nurses, home care staff and general practitioners from one municipality reported 21 cases during a six-month period (Saveman and Hallberg, 1997).

To summarise, the main results from the Scandinavian studies of elder abuse in a family context do not differ much from other findings. The abused people were elderly, mostly women and with no clear pattern of physical and/or psychological impairment. The abusers were mostly close relatives, with and without caring responsibility. The relationships between the parties were in some cases characterised by long-lasting conflict. Mental disturbances, alcohol abuse and financial problems were reported as contributing to the abuse. There was often a combination of various types of abuse – including psychological abuse, which was most commonly reported.

There seems to be a need for more research and for practical implementations in all the countries reviewed. Even if the phenomenon of elder abuse varies enormously according to context, some common needs have emerged:

- greater public awareness and more research about elder abuse in institutions and residential care;
- education and greater knowledge among professionals on how to deal with the problem.

Elder abuse – a problem in residential settings?

Abusive acts in residential settings are closely related to the quality of care generally as well as being an ethical concern of good/bad and right/wrong. Therefore the responsibility of staff to treat older people with dignity and respect are important factors in the quality of care given. Quality assurance programmes, standards and norms are developed in almost every caring organisation. However, this will not lead to good quality of care unless staff are familiar with what is good and right in their daily relationship with people in their care.

There are suggestions that several key factors are related to elder abuse in residential homes (Pillemer, 1988; Wierucka and Goodridge, 1996). These include the environment of the residential setting and the characteristics of the staff (Pillemer and Bachman-Prehn, 1991) – for example, their educational level, 'burn-out' and staff turn-over – as well as the characteristics of the residents. Physical demands and communication difficulties such as cognitive impairment have been related to maltreatment and abuse (Pillemer and Moore, 1989; Coyne et al, 1993; Fulmer and Gurland, 1996). Gilleard (1994) has discussed these key factors and concluded that the best predictors seem to be resident (patient) characteristics and staff burn-out:

If certain patients contribute more to burn-out than others this may set up a vicious circle: patients with the greatest mental and physical infirmity are most exhausting to care for; are therefore most likely to induce professional depersonalisation in those who care for them; and thus are at increased risk of both individual acts of abuse and more pervasively abusive practices from the staff. (Gilleard, 1994, p 107)

The relatively small number of studies on abuse in nursing or residential care have revealed mutual assaults between staff and residents (Coyne et al, 1993), staff being assaulted by residents (Lee-Treweek, 1994; Goodridge et al, 1996) and, finally, abuse of residents by staff (Pillemer and Moore, 1989, 1990; Pillemer and Bachman-Prehn, 1991; Beaulieu, 1992; Meddaugh, 1993; Fulmer and Gurland, 1996; Saveman et al, 1999).

In the USA, psychological abuse by almost 600 nursing home staff investigated seemed to be very common (Pillemer and Moore, 1989, 1990). As many as 40 per cent of the staff admitted to psychological abuse and 10 per cent to at least one physical act against the patients. Verbal abuse (such as infantilisation), lack of attention to the needs of the residents, threats and ignoring are related to the interaction between staff and the older person. When, for example, an older person has aggressive behaviour, the reaction by staff might be, if not physical, some kind of verbal abuse. Almost one-third of the respondents in Pillemer and Moore's study (1989) reported daily conflict with their patients. 'Circular' violence was reported to be high; 90 per cent of staff had been subjected to verbal and physical abuse by the patients, and almost half of them reported observing various kinds of abuse on several occasions. It was reported in another study that staff could expect to be physically assaulted by residents on average nine times per month and verbally assaulted eleven times (Goodridge et al, 1996).

Staff burn-out, residents' aggression and staff–resident conflicts are said to be related to each other (Cooper and Mendonca, 1989; Goodridge et al, 1996) and to psychological abuse (Pillemer and Bachman-Prehn, 1991). Attitudes to work, burn-out and stress, and attitudes to patients, as well as patient aggression, were aspects highlighted in describing difficulties in nursing home care related to elder abuse (Pillemer and Moore, 1990).

Violence and care in residential settings – an ongoing Swedish research project

A Swedish research project has begun that aims to uncover the violence occurring between staff and residents (both assault on staff and elder abuse) in residential settings. In the first study, 500 staff members (registered nurses, enrolled nurses and nursing aides) in two municipalities in Sweden answered a questionnaire concerning violence in residential settings (Saveman et al, 1999). The response rate in this study was almost 80 per cent, indicating an interest in unveiling elder abuse and its consequent problems. Included in the study are staff who work in older people's own homes, so reports of abusive acts include relatives as the abusers.

Eleven per cent of the nursing staff knew of elder abuse and 2 per cent admitted that they themselves had used violence against a resident during the last year. Most of those who reported elder abuse were enrolled nurses and nursing aides. More than two-thirds of the staff who reported elder abuse worked in nursing homes. Other staff members were reported to be the abusers by more than 70 per cent of the nursing staff. Some of them reported both other staff members and relatives.

Often, more than one type of abuse was reported in any given situation. Of the staff responding, 80 per cent reported physical and psychological abuse, followed by 60 per cent reporting neglect and maltreatment. Only one staff member was aware of sexual abuse. Nine of the staff said that psychological abuse happened daily and 19 reported that it happened some time every week. Physical abuse was reported as happening some time per week and some time per month by one-fifth of the staff who responded to the questionnaire. Feelings such as powerlessness, anger towards the abuser and compassion for the abused person were reported. In order to cope, staff talked to each other or to the manager. They recommended more education and support as main preventive strategies.

These results (Saveman et al, 1999) seem to be the first in Scandinavia in which nursing staff report elder abuse in residential settings including staff as the abusers. Tornstam (1989) reported that 20 per cent of a random sample of adults were aware of staff being abusive towards an older person in her or his own home.

Elder abuse and interventions

In Norway the main intervention work has been to implement the idea of Adult Protective Service from the USA. In one part of Oslo, a two-year pilot project for 'Elder Protective Service' has been completed. Its aim was to promote inter-disciplinary and inter-agency co-operation when dealing with elder abuse in people's own homes. A social worker functioned as mediator between the abused and the various professionals who were engaged to help. This social worker was a key person who co-ordinated the interventions, focused on the clients' needs. To be able to concentrate on getting in touch with, as well as to mediate adequate help to, the elderly victim is one strength associated with this kind of intervention. The more frail and helpless the abused elders are, the more important this kind of intervention is. The positive results from the project have been implemented in Oslo as well as elsewhere in Norway (Johns et al, 1994).

In the Netherlands, help centres have been developed where abused people and professionals can seek assistance. The aim is to identify how big the problem is, to overcome the taboo concerning elder abuse and to find ways to initiate help for the victims. The government has allocated financial assistance for research, including a practical project (Jansen, 1995).

In the early 1990s no support was available in Sweden to the district nurses who, as witnesses and helpers, described considerable problems in dealing with abuse of the elderly. They attempted to strike a balance between active and passive strategies or, in their own words, 'walking a fine line' when approaching, recognising (ie identifying, defining, judging), diagnosing and intervening in abusive families. Through all these steps the district nurses could have chosen to distance themselves had they so wished. They experienced negative feelings such as powerlessness and uncertainty, which, with few support facilities available, led to a conflict of loyalties. They also had problems in managing their own feelings, thoughts, wishes and actions, which reduced the possibilities of intervening constructively (Saveman et al, 1992).

Interventions suggested by physicians, nurses and home care staff in hypothetical cases of abuse were investigated in a Swedish study (Saveman and Hallberg, 1997). Their suggestions were placed in one of three groups:

● limited intervention, mostly of a social type (eg care services);
● more specific intervention relating to health care and voluntary use (eg referring the abuser to an alcohol treatment centre);
● all types of intervention (not necessarily specific to the case).

The type of intervention proposed seemed to depend on the individual situation and on the profession or organisation making the proposal.

For a long time the Swedish authorities, as in other European countries, have done little about either implementing the recommendations made by researchers or complying with suggested guidelines and interventions. In 1996, however, a recommendation from the National Board of Health and Welfare was implemented in Sweden: it says that all staff working with older people should report to the local authority any cases of elder abuse. It also gives recommendations to the municipalities on what to do when cases are detected and reported (National Board of Health and Welfare, 1996).

The results from the Swedish study of hypothetical cases and proposed interventions indicated that the various professionals might have different views underlying their strategies (Saveman and Hallberg, 1997). Working together might be of help both to the professionals and to the abused person, but the findings revealed that such co-operation does not always occur. Nevertheless, systematic supervision and support from colleagues might help to find solutions at the meta level, which otherwise would be difficult for an individual to discern when involved as a witness and a helper in the specific situation. Most important, however, is that information gathering and education must be never-ending.

Pillemer and Hudson (1993) evaluated the results of a training programme for the prevention of abuse in residential settings. They found that staff felt powerless, but the training programme gave them the opportunity to talk openly about the problem of elder abuse, with the effect that the self-reported abusive actions and conflicts with the residents declined. There seems to be a general need among nursing staff for increased understanding and competence in dealing with elder abuse (cf Saveman et al, 1992; Saveman, 1994).

Recommendations and guidelines – an EU-funded collaboration

An EU-funded collaboration among British, Swedish and Spanish authorities was undertaken during 1996/97 to exchange expertise about the residential care of older people, to identify factors related to abuse, to evaluate preventive strategies and to present recommendations and guidelines. An underlying assumption was that, as with elder abuse in a family context, there must be some general issues about elder abuse in residential care. Another assumption was that there is need internationally for recommendations and guidelines, as several research studies and individual professionals in this area have identified a lack of guidance.

The results that emerged after visiting and observing residential care and services for older people in each country concerned the size of the home/unit, the residents' level of choice and influence, the documentation held by the establishment, the level and type of staff training, management and peer support, and visitors coming to the homes. The interim conclusions in the report are:

- the active and explicit promotion of quality of life generally;
- the specific recognition that elder abuse can still occur as well as be detected and stopped;
- lessons will be learned to further improve the quality of care and service in residential settings.

These recommendations and accompanying guidelines are based on the underpinning values of treating older people with respect and dignity, giving them choices and respecting their individual integrity as well as allowing them to remain independent as long as possible. They are also based on an awareness that, because staff working with older people can face difficult tasks, with high work-loads and running the risk of burn-out and isolation, they need specific education and supervision. Staff should establish good relationships based on respect and dignity for the residents. Therefore, the attitudes of staff, their education and supervision as well as a peer review system are important factors. In order to promote appropriate attitudes (eg towards violence, ageism, gender and responsibilities), training and group supervision with a focus on quality of care and service are recommended.

It is also recommended that residential settings have an open and inviting atmosphere so that, for example, family, friends and people from voluntary organisations feel free to visit and help. It is well known that isolation is a factor in elder abuse, in that isolation offers opportunities for abusive behaviour as well as a way to hide abuse. Involvement of outsiders in the life of the care home is also important. Voluntary organisations, religious organisations, family carers and so on should be involved in the care and service if the resident so wishes.

The recommendations pertaining to quality of care include standards for care and service, inspection rounds and keeping appropriate records. Individual social, medical and nursing care plans are of great importance and help to ensure continuity and good quality care.

Finally, the recommendations and guidelines should be seen as a summary of important aspects in the prevention of elder abuse in residential care. They are founded on residents' needs for good quality care and service as well as providing the means for highlighting the topic of elder abuse and neglect in residential care (Eastman et al, 1997).

Implications for practice

One might ask what implications and suggestions can be drawn from the literature review. From an ethical perspective, it can be seen that professional carers have problems in knowing how to act in a good and proper manner. On the whole, they feel uncertain and do not know whether a particular intervention is correct. A care worker who has been subjected to abusive behaviour or shows abusive behaviour towards a resident might experience both anger and a sense of degradation simultaneously with feelings of shame and guilt. There seems to be a need for norms and guidelines, for example, with regard to intervention strategies in specific cases, as well as the possibility of having someone with whom to discuss such problems.

It is difficult to summarise clearly what was suggested by the theoretical knowledge as it was translated from policy to practice. Nevertheless, it is of the utmost importance to focus first on the relationship between the parties involved, such as the older person, the family member and the staff. Secondly, it should be remembered that abusive behaviour is often a combination of at least two types of abuse: psychological and another. Thirdly, it is important to note the negative feelings reported by staff members involved in abusive acts. Recommendations and guidelines, supervision, regular staff meetings and training courses are examples of intervention strategies needed. Finally, the ethical and moral responsibilities involved in all caring relationships must be highlighted. It is the needs of the older people – in society at large and in residential settings – that are of prime importance when staff members provide care for them.

There is an ethical and moral dimension underpinning norms and rules in, for example, a residential setting. When people interact and relate to each other positively there is a fundamental trust and human love between them, which fosters good actions. However, this is not always the case. Sometimes the trust and love are perverted into mistrust, cruelty and mistreatment. In such cases we need to draw on our life experience and personal development to know what is the good and right thing to do. Norms and rules are developed in society in order to help maintain good relationships without confrontations. In cases of elder abuse, staff may be involved in or confronted by situations of which many of them have no earlier experience. Therefore, recommendations and guidelines are important in helping individuals to act in a good and right manner when dealing with prevention, detection and handling of abusive situations (Saveman, 1994).

Work on finding good and right ways to intervene in cases of elder abuse, whether in people's own homes or in residential settings, takes time – probably because this issue has been accorded low priority. The complexity of the abusive situations, the various professional perspectives and research designs all point to a need for more collaboration and inter-disciplinary exchange of experiences. Because older abused people often need help from more than one authority, they run the risk of falling between two stools. In Sweden the health and welfare system is based on various specialities, and there is a risk that none of these specialities will assume full responsibility. This may well be the case elsewhere. In many countries local government is responsible for the provision of both health care and social services to older people. Having a local government official, or mediator, interested in the topic could help not only the abused person but also the professionals involved.

The low priority given to elder abuse is in line with how older people are often treated in the health care and social services systems in many countries. If you are old and your problems are complex and you do not have the strength to state your needs, you might risk not being taken seriously and not being considered a high priority.

The various research results have one thing in common: elder abuse exists even if there are no precise figures of the number of people affected by it. Both practical knowledge of how to deal with abusive situations and more research into its causes and possible prevention are needed. It seems unethical not to intervene in cases of abuse, because abuse causes suffering. Taking responsibility for intervention is of great ethical/moral concern for all who are involved in older people's health and welfare.

Conclusion

Phil Slater and Mervyn Eastman

It is customary at the end of a theoretical text to provide at least a brief conclusion, not by way of summarising the detailed arguments that have been elaborated in the preceding chapters but by distilling the essential themes that have emerged throughout the book as a whole. Such a conclusion would be doubly relevant in the case of an edited text of diverse authorship, particularly when the selection of contributors is extended beyond the narrow confines of academia. As the Introduction advised, editorial policy was not merely to accommodate heterogeneous writing styles but also to tolerate repetition of detail and even divergence of opinion.

Nevertheless, individual chapters were commissioned on the basis of a common 'critical' programme, the meaning of which was elaborated on at some length in the Introduction, along with brief summaries of the chapters that followed. The role of a conclusion in this context is merely to distil the essential themes that have emerged in the execution of the original brief. However, given the authors' shared concern not merely to comment on but also to actively intervene in what has become known as 'the social construction of an elder abuse problem', these themes are most appropriately expressed as a set of critical objectives that will, hopefully, inform future collaborative endeavour. These objectives can be provisionally formulated as follows.

- Explicit location of elder abuse within the social relations of later life, with central reference to financial status and gender relations.
- Conscious disengagement from ageist ideologies and stereotypes, specifically as regards assumptions of global incapacity.

- Reasoned argument for and against demarcation of elder abuse from the abuse/neglect of other 'vulnerable' groups; for example, adults with learning difficulties.
- Sustained vigilance against diminished expectations of older people subjected to abuse/neglect, as compared with, say, younger women experiencing domestic violence.
- Proactive integration of research into elder abuse in the domestic setting on the one hand and residential/nursing accommodation on the other.
- Detailed assessment of existing and prospective legislative provision, with particular reference to the balance of rights, risks, restrictions and redress.
- Multi-disciplinary transcendence of competing models of elder abuse intervention, ranging from medical 'pathology/treatment' to social 'care/protection'.
- Progressive restructuring of power relations among politicians, professionals, charities and users/carers, at the complementary levels of policy formulation and direct practice.

The formulation of these objectives is acknowledged as provisional: their purpose would best be served by provoking critical scrutiny and collaborative revision across the widest possible socio-political spectrum.

The ultimately political nature of the 'social construction' of elder abuse was dramatically underlined in 1998, when the British government initiated a public consultation exercise on a Green Paper entitled *Who Decides? Making decisions on behalf of mentally incapacitated adults* (Lord Chancellor's Department, 1997). In line with the enhanced brief of the Law Commission's pioneering work in this area (which has been commented on at length in the present book), the Green Paper also considered the issue of statutory protection for 'people at risk' generally. Specifically, it noted that 'a number of initiatives have been undertaken to address the particular problem of elder abuse, and these cannot yet be fully evaluated' (p 68).

A major message of the present collaborative work is that previous and current initiatives concerned with elder abuse should be critically evaluated with reference to their impact at the political interface between individuals, groups and the state. More importantly, prospective initiatives need to be proactively formulated and justified in similar terms. Thereby, a contemplative stance is superseded by what the young Karl Marx termed the 'practical-critical' standpoint (Marx, 1845/1976, p 3). Suitably adapted, Marx's accompanying aphorism can serve as a convenient conclusion to this book: the evaluators have only *interpreted* the world in various ways, while the point is to *change* it.

APPENDIX:
MODERNISING SOCIAL SERVICES

Completion of this book's editing stage coincided with the publication of an important White Paper, *Modernising Social Services* (Department of Health, 1998), carrying major implications for the recognition, prevention and tackling of elder abuse. Asking the authors to update their chapters in the light of this White Paper would have delayed the publishing timetable, so it was agreed to proceed with production, but to add this Appendix, at the last possible moment.

The key themes of the White Paper are indicated in its subtitle:

- promoting independence;
- improving protection;
- raising standards.

The specific concern with improvements to the protection of vulnerable people is related to the phenomenon of elder abuse, albeit with exclusive reference to situations in which the perpetrators are service employees. Thus, while 'any decent society' owes to its elderly citizens 'the right to live in dignity, free from fear of abuse', it is well documented that many elderly people 'have been exposed to neglect and abuse by the very people who were supposed to care for them' (p 5).

Efforts to remedy this situation are mounted on a number of fronts, including care staff training and registration. However, the strategic focus is on service regulation: 'no regulatory system can absolutely guarantee consistently good standards everywhere, but we must make sure that the system we put in place does everything that is possible to prevent and root out the abuse and neglect of vulnerable people' (p 64).

Specific reforms comprise:

- the establishment of regional Commissions for Care Standards – independent authorities responsible solely for the regulation of care services;

- the extension of regulation to services not already covered by existing arrangements, most notably domiciliary services;
- the promotion of greater consistency in standards across the care sector, coupled with greater effectiveness in complaints, inspection and enforcement procedures.

Taken in conjunction with the other initiatives flagged up in the White Paper as a whole, such reforms will help create a society in which, in the words of its conclusion, 'everyone will be safeguarded against abuse, neglect or poor treatment while receiving care' (p 125).

Such a focus is, of course, organisationally distinct from the related question of 'public law protection' for vulnerable adults, the prospects for which have been systematically considered by the Law Commission and covered extensively in the present book. At the time of going to press, the Government's last word on this score was that, while there 'may be merit in some of the recommendations made in this area', it is 'not convinced that there is a pressing need for reform' (Lord Chancellor's Department, 1997, p 68).

REFERENCES

INTRODUCTION

Aitken L, Griffin G (1996) *Gender Issues in Elder Abuse*. Sage, London.

Bennett G, Kingston P (1993) *Elder Abuse: Concepts, theories and interventions*. Chapman & Hall, London.

Bennett G, Kingston P, Penhale B (1997) *The Dimensions of Elder Abuse: Perspectives for practitioners*. Macmillan, Basingstoke.

Berlin I (1969) *Four Essays on Liberty*. Oxford University Press, London.

Biggs S (1997) 'Social policy as elder abuse', in P Decalmer and F Glendenning (eds) *The Mistreatment of Elderly People*, 2nd edition. Sage, London.

Blumer H (1971) 'Social problems as collective behavior', *Social Problems*, 18(3): 298–306.

Decalmer P, Glendenning F (eds) (1997) *The Mistreatment of Elderly People*, 2nd edition. Sage, London.

Department of Health (1995) *Child Protection: Messages from research*. HMSO, London.

Eastman M (ed) (1994) *Old Age Abuse: A new perspective*, 2nd edition. Chapman & Hall, London.

Jack R (ed) (1995) *Empowerment in Community Care*. Chapman & Hall, London.

Kingston P, Penhale B (eds) (1995) *Family Violence and the Caring Professions*. Macmillan, Basingstoke.

Leroux T, Petrunik M (1990) 'The construction of elder abuse as a social problem: a Canadian experience', *International Journal of Health Services*, 20(4): 651–663.

McCreadie C (1991) *Elder Abuse: An exploratory study*. Age Concern Institute of Gerontology, London.

McCreadie C (1996) *Elder Abuse: Update on research*, Age Concern Institute of Gerontology, London.

North S (1997) 'Dissenting voices', *Community Care*, 1–7 May: 22.

Wolf R, Pillemer K (1989) *Helping Elderly Victims: The reality of elder abuse*. Columbia University Press, New York.

1 RESEARCHING ELDER ABUSE: LESSONS FOR PRACTICE

Action on Elder Abuse (1995) *Everybody's Business: Taking action on elder abuse*. AEA, London.

Barron B, Cran A, Flitcroft J et al (1990) *No Innocent Bystanders: A study of abuse of older people in our community*. Office of Public Advocate, Melbourne.

Beneito A, Eastman M, Guijarro A et al (1997) *Abuse of Older People in Residential Care: A European project*. London Borough of Enfield, London.

Bennett G, Kingston P, Penhale B (1997) *The Dimensions of Elder Abuse: Perspectives for practitioners*. Macmillan, Basingstoke.

Chelucci K, Coyle J (1992) *Elder Abuse Acute Care Resource Manual*. Elder Abuse Specialists, Toledo, Ohio.

Commijs H, Jonker C, Smit JH (1997) 'Hostility and Coping Styles as Risk Factors of Elder Abuse'. Paper given at 16th World Congress of Gerontology, Adelaide.

Compton SA, Flanigan P, Gregg W (1997) 'Elder abuse in people with dementia in Northern Ireland: prevalence and predictors in cases referred to a Psychiatry of Old Age Service', *International Journal of Geriatric Psychiatry*, 12: 632–635.

Cooney C, Mortimer A (1995) 'Elder abuse and dementia – a pilot study', *International Journal of Social Psychiatry*, 41(4): 276–283.

Coyne A, Reichman WE, Berbig LJ (1993) 'The relationship between dementia and elder abuse', *American Journal of Psychiatry*, 150(4): 643–646.

Department of Health (1995) *Child Protection: Messages from research*. HMSO, London.

Diba R (1996) *Meeting the Costs of Continuing Care: Public views and perceptions*. Joseph Rowntree Foundation, York.

Grafström M, Norberg A, Wimblad B (1992) 'Abuse is in the eye of the beholder. Reports by family members about abuse of demented persons in home care. A total population-based study', *Scandinavian Journal of Social Medicine*, 21(4): 247–255.

Heinanen A (ed) (1986) *The Elderly and Family Violence*, Report of the Federation of Mother–Child Homes and Shelters, No 8. FMCHS, Helsinki.

Homer A, Gilleard C (1990) 'Abuse of elderly people by their carers'. *British Medical Journal*, 301: 1359–1362.

Homer A, Gilleard C (1994) 'The effect of in-patient respite care on elderly patients and their carers', *Age & Ageing*, 23: 274–276.

Hydle I, Johns S (1992) *Closed Doors and Clenched Fists: When elderly people are abused in their homes*. Kommuneforlaget, Oslo.

Johns S, Hydle I, Aschjem O (1991) 'The act of abuse: a two-headed monster of injury and offence', *Journal of Elder Abuse & Neglect*, 3(1): 53–64.

Johns S (1993) 'Family Life and Solidarity across the Generations'. Paper delivered at the Annual Conference of the British Society of Gerontology, University of East Anglia, September.

Kingston P, Penhale B (eds) (1995) *Family Violence and the Caring Professions*. Macmillan, Basingstoke.

Kingston P, Penhale B, Bennett G (1995) 'Is elder abuse on the curriculum?: the relative contribution of child abuse, domestic violence and elder abuse in social work, nursing and medical qualifying curricula', *Health and Social Care in the Community*, 3(6): 353–362.

Kivelä SL, Köngäs-Saviaro P, Kesti E et al (1992) 'Abuse in old age – epidemiological data from Finland', *Journal of Elder Abuse & Neglect*, 4(3):1–18.

Kurrle SE (1993a) 'Elder abuse: a hidden problem', *Modern Medicine of Australia*, 58–71.

Kurrle SE (1993b) 'Responding to elder abuse. I: Cases and interventions: responding to elder abuse – a follow-up study of interventions and outcomes'. *Australian Journal on Ageing*, 12(4): 5–9.

Kurrle SE (1993c) 'Responding to elder abuse. II: A review of developments', *Australian Journal on Ageing*, 12(4): 24–31.

Kurrle SE, Sadler PM, Cameron ID (1991) 'Elder abuse – an Australian case series', *Medical Journal of Australia*, 155: 150–153.

Kurrle SE, Sadler PM, Cameron ID (1992) 'Patterns of elder abuse', *Medical Journal of Australia*, 157: 673–676.

Law Commission (1991) *Mentally Incapacitated Adults and Decision Making: An overview*, Consultation Paper No 119. London, HMSO.

Law Commission (1993a) *Mentally Incapacitated Adults: A New Jurisdiction*, Consultation Paper No 128. HMSO, London.

Law Commission (1993b) *Mentally Incapacitated Adults: Medical treatment and research*, Consultation Paper No 129. HMSO, London.

Law Commission (1993c) *Mentally Incapacitated and Other Vulnerable Adults: Public law protection*, Consultation Paper No 130. HMSO, London.

Law Commission (1995) *Mental Incapacity*, Report No 231. HMSO, London.

McCallum J (1993) 'Elder abuse: the "new" social problem?', *Modern Medicine of Australia*, September, 74–83.

McCallum J, Matiasz S, Graycar A (1990) *Abuse of the Elderly at Home: The range of the problem*. Office of the Commissioner of Ageing, Adelaide.

McCreadie C (1995) *A Guide to Elder Abuse Research in the UK*. Action on Elder Abuse, London.

McCreadie C (1996) *Elder Abuse: An update on research*. HMSO, London.

McCreadie C, Bennett G, Tinker A (1998) 'Working together: report of research on general practitioners and elder abuse', *Health and Social Care in the Community*, 6(6): 464–467.

McDermott J (1993) 'Elder Abuse' – eight scenarios in search of a construct'. Paper presented at the Crime and Older People Conference, Adelaide.

Ogg J (1993) 'Researching elder abuse in Britain', *Journal of Elder Abuse & Neglect*, 5(2): 37–54.

Ogg J, Bennett G (1992) 'Elder abuse in Britain', *British Medical Journal*, 305: 998–999.

Penhale B (1993) 'The abuse of elderly people: considerations for practice', *British Journal of Social Work*, 23(3): 96–112.

Pot AM, van Dyck R, Jonker C, Deeg DJH (1996) 'Verbal and physical aggression against demented elderly by informal caregivers in the Netherlands', *Journal of Social Psychiatry and Social Epidemiology*, 31(3-4): 156–162.

Rowe J, Davies K, Baburaj V, Sinha R (1993) 'F.A.D.E. A.W.A.Y. The financial affairs of the dementing elderly and who is the attorney?' *Journal of Elder Abuse & Neglect*, 5(2): 73–79.

Sadler P, Kurrle S, Cameron I (1995) 'Dementia and elder abuse', *Australian Journal on Ageing*, 14(1): 36–40.

Saveman B-I (1994) Formal Carers in Health Care and the Social Services Witnessing Abuse of the Elderly in their Homes. Umeå University, Dissertation (unpublished).

Saveman B-I, Norberg A (1993) 'Cases of elder abuse: intervention and hopes for the future, as reported by home service personnel', *Scandinavian Journal of Caring Science*, 7: 21–28.

Saveman B-I, Hallberg IR, Norberg A, Eriksson S (1993) 'Patterns of abuse of the elderly in their homes as reported by district nurses', *Scandinavian Journal of Primary Health Care*, 11: 111–116.

Taylor S (1989) 'How prevalent is it?', in W Stainton Rodgers, D Hevey and E Ash (eds) *Child Abuse and Neglect: Facing the challenge*. Open University Press/Batsford, London.

Tornstam L (1989) 'Abuse of the elderly in Denmark and Sweden. Results from a population study', *Journal of Elder Abuse & Neglect*, 1(1): 35–44.

Troke A (1994) 'Financial abuse', *Action on Elder Abuse Bulletin*, 8.

van Weeghel J, Faber E (1995) 'Reporting Elderly Abuse'. Paper given at the European Congress of Gerontology, Amsterdam.

Weiss J (1988) 'Family violence research methodology and design', in L Ohlin and M Tonry (eds) *Family Violence*. University of Chicago Press, Chicago.

2 PUTTING ELDER ABUSE ON THE AGENDA: ACHIEVEMENTS OF A CAMPAIGN

Action on Elder Abuse (1997) *Annual Report 1996–1997*. AEA, London.

Action on Elder Abuse/Family Policy Studies Centre (1997) *Hearing the Despair: The reality of elder abuse*. AEA, London.

Age Concern England (1986) *The Law and Vulnerable Elderly People*. ACE, Mitcham.

Age Concern England (1991) *The National Policy*. ACE, London.

Age Concern, British Association of Social Workers, British Geriatrics Society et al (undated) *Abuse of Elderly People: Guidelines for action*. Age Concern England, London

Aitken L, Griffin G (1996) *Gender Issues in Elder Abuse*. Sage, London.

Baumann E (1989) 'Research rhetoric and the social construction of elder abuse', in J Best (ed) *Images of Issues: Typifying contemporary problems*. de Gruyter, New York.

Bennett G, Kingston P, Penhale B (1997) *Dimensions of Elder Abuse*. Macmillan, London.

Biggs S (1997) 'Social policy as elder abuse', in P Decalmer and F Glendenning (eds) *The Mistreatment of Elderly People*. Sage, London.

Blumer H (1971) 'Social problems as collective behaviour', *Social Problems*, 18(3): 298–306.

Cloke C (1983) *Old Age Abuse in the Domestic Setting: A review*. ACE, Mitcham.

Dalley G (1989) 'Professional ideology or organisational tribalism? The health service–social work divide', in J Walmsley, J Reynolds, P Shakespeare and R Woolfe (eds) *Health, Welfare and Practice: Reflecting on roles and relationships*. Sage, London.

Davis Smith J, Rochester C, Hedley R (eds) (1995) *An Introduction to the Voluntary Sector*. Routledge, London.

Decalmer P, Glendenning F (eds) (1993) *The Mistreatment of Elderly People*. Sage, London.

Decalmer P, Glendenning F (eds) (1997) *The Mistreatment of Elderly People*, 2nd edition. Sage, London.

Eastman M (1984) *Old Age Abuse*. Age Concern England, Mitcham.

Eastman M (ed) (1994) *Old Age Abuse: A new perspective*. Chapman & Hall/Age Concern England, London.

Ginn J (1993) 'Grey power: age-based organisations' response to structured inequalities', *Critical Social Policy*, 38: 23–47.

Hogwood B, Gurr L (1984) *Policy Analysis for the Real World*. Oxford University Press, Oxford.

Hugman R (1995) 'The implications of the term "elder abuse" for problem definition and response in health and social welfare', *Journal of Social Policy*, 24(4): 493–508.

Kearns K (1997) 'Social democratic perspectives on the welfare state', in M Lavalette and A Pratt (eds) *Social Policy: A conceptual and theoretical introduction*. Sage, London.

Law Commission (1991) *Decision Making and the Mentally Incapacitated Adult*, Consultation Paper No 119. HMSO, London.

Law Commission (1993) *Mentally Incapacitated and Other Vulnerable Adults: Public law protection*, Consultation Paper No 130. HMSO, London.

Law Commission (1995) *Mental Incapacity*, Report No 231. HMSO, London.

Leroux T, Petrunik M (1990) 'The construction of elder abuse as a social problem: a Canadian perspective', *International Journal of Health Services*, 20(4): 651–663.

Levin P (1997) *Making Social Policy*. Open University Press, Buckingham.

Manthorpe J, Stanley N, Bradley G, Alaszewski A (1996) 'Working together effectively', *Health Care in Later Life*, 1(3): 143–155.

Penhale B, Kingston P (1995) 'Social perspectives on elder abuse', in P Kingston and B Penhale (eds) *Family Violence and the Caring Professions*. Macmillan, London.

Phillipson C, Biggs S (1995) 'Elder abuse: a critical overview', in P Kingston and B Penhale (eds) *Family Violence and the Caring Professions*. Macmillan, London.

Public Concern at Work (1997) *A Review of the Activities of Public Concern at Work*. PCW, London.

Social Services Inspectorate/Department of Health (1993) *No Longer Afraid: The safeguard of older people in domestic settings*. HMSO, London.

Whitmore R (1984) 'Modelling the policy/implementation distinction: the case of child abuse', *Policy and Politics*, 12: 241–267.

Whittaker T (1997) 'Rethinking elder abuse: towards an age and gender integrated theory of elder abuse', in P Decalmer and F Glendenning (eds) *The Mistreatment of Elderly People*, 2nd edition, Sage, London.

3 ELDER ABUSE AS HARM TO OLDER ADULTS: THE RELEVANCE OF AGE

Action on Elder Abuse (1995) *Everybody's Business: Taking action on elder abuse*. AEA, London.

Age Concern England (1986) *The Law and Vulnerable Elderly People*. ACE, Mitcham.

Ambache J, Davey I (1997) 'Towards a national framework for tackling adult abuse', *Professional Social Work*, November: 20.

Ashton G (1994) 'Action on elder abuse: has it got its focus right?', *Action on Elder Abuse Bulletin*, 6: 1–3.

Association of Directors of Social Services (1991) *Adults at Risk: Guidance for directors of social services*. ADSS, Stockport.

Association of Directors of Social Services (1995) *Mistreatment of Older People: A discussion document*, ADSS, Northallerton.

Baumhover L, Beall S (eds) (1996) *Abuse, Neglect and Exploitation of Older Persons: Strategies for assessment and intervention*. Jessica Kingsley, London.

Bennett G, Kingston P (1993) *Elder Abuse: Concepts, theories and interventions*. Chapman & Hall, London.

Biggs S, Phillipson C, Kingston P (1995) *Elder Abuse in Perspective*. Open University Press, Buckingham.

Blumer H (1971) 'Social problems as collective behavior', *Social Problems*, 18(3): 298–306.

Breckman R, Adelman R (1988) *Strategies for Helping Victims of Elder Mistreatment*. Sage, Newbury Park.

Bytheway B (1995) *Ageism*. Open University Press, Buckingham.

Counsel and Care (1992) *What If They Hurt Themselves?* Counsel and Care, London.

Crystal S (1986) 'Social policy and elder abuse', in K Pillemer and R Wolf (eds) *Elder Abuse: Conflict in the family*. Dover/Auburn House, Massachusetts.

Decalmer P, Glendenning F (eds) (1993) *The Mistreatment of Elderly People*. Sage, London.

Department of Health (1993) *No Longer Afraid: The safeguard of older people in domestic settings*. HMSO, London.

Department of Health (1995) *Abuse of Older People in Domestic Settings: A report on two SSI seminars*. DoH, London.

Eastman M (1984) *Old Age Abuse*. Age Concern England, Mitcham.

Eastman M (ed) (1994) *Old Age Abuse: A new perspective*. Age Concern England/Chapman & Hall, London.

Finkelhor D, Pillemer K (1988) 'Elder abuse: its relationship to other forms of domestic violence', in G Hotaling et al (eds) *Family Abuse and its Consequences: New directions in research*. Sage, Newbury Park.

Hughes B (1995) *Older People and Community Care: Critical theory and practice*. Open University Press, Buckingham.

Hugman R (1995) 'The implications of the term "elder abuse" for problem definition and response in health and social welfare', *Journal of Social Policy*, 24(4):493–507.

Iveson C (1990) *Whose Life? Community care of older people and their families*. BT Press, London.

Kingston P, Penhale B (eds) (1995) *Family Violence and the Caring Professions*. Macmillan, Basingstoke.

Law Commission (1991) *Mentally Incapacitated Adults and Decision Making: An overview*, Consultation Paper No 119. HMSO, London.

Law Commission (1993) *Mentally Incapacitated and Other Vulnerable Adults: Public law protection*, Consultation Paper No 130. HMSO, London.

Law Commission (1995) *Mental Incapacity*, Report No 231. HMSO, London.

Lord Chancellor's Department (1997) *Who Decides? Making decisions on behalf of mentally incapacitated adults*, Cm 3803. HMSO, London.

Manthorpe J (1997) 'Developing social work practice in protection and assistance', in P Decalmer and F Glendenning (eds) *The Mistreatment of Elderly People*, 2nd edition. Sage, London.

McCreadie C (1991) *Elder Abuse: An exploratory study*. Age Concern Institute of Gerontology, London.

McCreadie C (1996) *Elder Abuse: Update on research*. Age Concern Institute of Gerontology, London.

Murray N (1993) 'Legal clout', *Community Care*, 1 July: 16–17.

North S (1997) 'Dissenting voices', *Community Care*, 1–7 May: 22.

Ogg J, Munn-Giddings C (1993) 'Researching elder abuse', *Ageing and Society*, 13(3): 389–413.

Penhale B (1993) 'Local authority guidelines and procedures', in C McCreadie (ed) *Elder Abuse: New findings and policy guidelines.* Age Concern Institute of Gerontology, London.

Penhale B, Kingston P (1995) 'Elder abuse: an overview of recent and current developments', *Health and Social Care in the Community*, 3(5): 311–320.

Pritchard J (1992) *The Abuse of Elderly People: A handbook for professionals.* Jessica Kingsley, London.

Scrutton S (1990) 'Ageism: the foundation of age discrimination', in E McEwen (ed) *Age: The unrecognised discrimination.* Age Concern England, London.

Slater P (1995) 'From "elder protection" to "adult empowerment": critical reflections on a UK campaign', in R Jack (ed) *Empowerment in Community Care.* Chapman & Hall, London.

Smale G, Tuson G, Ahmad B et al (1994) *Negotiating Care in the Community: The implications of research findings on community based practice for the implementation of the Community Care and Children Acts.* HMSO, London.

Steinmetz S (1990) 'Elder abuse: myth and reality', in T Brubaker (ed) *Family Relationships in Later Life*, 2nd edition. Sage, Newbury Park.

Stevenson O (1989) *Age and Vulnerability: A guide to better care.* Edward Arnold, London.

Stevenson O (1995) Foreword, in P Kingston and B Penhale (eds) *Family Violence and the Caring Professions.* Macmillan, Basingstoke.

Stevenson O (1996) 'Changing practice: professional attitudes, consumerism and empowerment', in R Bland (ed) *Developing Services for Older People and Their Families.* Jessica Kingsley, London.

Thomas M, Pierson J (eds) (1995) *Dictionary of Social Work.* Collins Educational, London.

Williams J (1995) 'Elder abuse: the legal framework', in R Clough (ed) *Elder Abuse and the Law.* Action on Elder Abuse, London.

Wolf R, Pillemer K (1989) *Helping Elderly Victims: The reality of elder abuse.* Columbia University Press, New York.

4 TACKLING ELDER ABUSE TOGETHER: DEVELOPING JOINT POLICIES AND PROCEDURES

Action on Elder Abuse (1995) *Everybody's Business: Taking action on elder abuse*. AEA, London.

Action on Elder Abuse (1996) *The Abuse of Older People at Home: Information for workers*. AEA, London.

Age Concern England (1986) *The Law and Vulnerable Elderly People*. ACE, London.

Association of Directors of Social Services (1991) *Adults at Risk*. ADSS, London.

Association of Directors of Social Services (1995) *Mistreatment of Older People: A discussion document*. ADSS, London.

Brown H, Stein J (1997) *Implementing Adult Protection Policies*. Open University School of Health and Welfare, Milton Keynes.

Brown H, Sangar V, Simpson L, Stein J (1996) 'The common enemy', *Community Care*, 2 May: 28–29.

Centre for Policy on Ageing (1984) *Home Life: A code of practice for residential care*. CPA, London.

Counsel and Care (1994) *Older people at risk of abuse in a residential setting*, Fact sheet 2. Counsel and Care, London.

Department of Health (1991) *Working Together under the Children Act 1989*. HMSO, London.

Department of Health (1997) *Better Management, Better Care*, the sixth annual report of the Chief Inspector of the Social Services Inspectorate 1996/7. Stationery Office, London.

Eastman M (1984) *Old Age Abuse*. Age Concern England, London.

Family Policy Studies Centre (1997) *Hearing the Despair: The reality of elder abuse*, a summary of the Elder Abuse Response Line Project. Action on Elder Abuse, London.

Langan J, Means R (1994) *Personal Finances, Elderly People with Dementia and the 'New' Community Care*. Anchor Housing Trust, Oxford.

Law Commission (1995) *Mental Incapacity*, Report No 231. HMSO, London.

McCreadie C (1991) *Elder Abuse: An exploratory study*. Age Concern Institute of Gerontology, London.

McCreadie C (1996a) *Elder Abuse: Update on research*. Age Concern Institute of Gerontology, London.

McCreadie C (ed) (1996b) *Elder Abuse: New perspectives and ways forward*, report of two Ageing Update Conferences. Age Concern Institute of Gerontology, London.

Penhale P (1993) 'Abuse on the map', *Community Care*, 10 June: 998–999.

Pritchard J (1995) *The Abuse of Older People*. Jessica Kingsley, London.

Social Services Inspectorate (1989) *Homes are for Living In*, updated 1993. HMSO, London.

Social Services Inspectorate (1992) *Confronting Elder Abuse*. HMSO, London.

Social Services Inspectorate (1993a) *No Longer Afraid: The safeguard of older people in domestic settings*. HMSO, London.

Social Services Inspectorate (1993b) *Developing Quality Standards for Home Support Services*. HMSO, London.

Social Services Inspectorate (1993c) *Inspecting for Quality: Standards for the residential care of elderly people with mental disorders*. HMSO, London.

Social Services Inspectorate (1995) *Abuse of Older People in Domestic Settings*, report on two SSI seminars. Department of Health, London.

Stevenson O (1996a) *Elder Protection in the Community: What can we learn from child protection?* Department of Health, London.

Stevenson O (1996b) in C McCreadie (ed) (1996b) *Elder Abuse: New perspectives and ways forward*, report of two Ageing Update Conferences. Age Concern Institute of Gerontology, London.

Wallis L (1997) 'The enforcers', *Guardian Weekend*, 24 May: 24–32.

5 ELDER ABUSE AND PARTICIPATION: A CRUCIAL COUPLING FOR CHANGE

Aitken L, Griffin G (1996) *Gender Issues in Elder Abuse.* Sage, London.

Baumhover LA, Beall SC (eds) (1996) *Abuse, Neglect and Exploitation of Older Persons: Strategies for assessment and intervention.* Jessica Kingsley, London.

Bennett G, Kingston P (1993) *Elder Abuse: Concepts, theories and interventions.* Chapman & Hall, London.

Beresford P (1988) 'Consumer views: data collection or democracy', in I White, M Devenney, R Bhaduri, J Barnes and A Jones (eds) *Hearing the Voice of the Consumer.* Policy Studies Institute, London.

Beresford P, Campbell J (1994) 'Disabled people, service users, user involvement and representation', *Disability and Society,* 9(3): 315–325.

Beresford P, Croft S (1978) *A Say in the Future: Planning, participation and meeting social need.* Battersea Community Action, London.

Beresford P, Croft S (1993) *Citizen Involvement: A practical guide for change.* Macmillan, Basingstoke.

Beresford P, Croft S, Evans C, Harding T (1997) 'Quality in personal social services: the developing role of user involvement in the UK', in A Evers, R Haverinen, K Leichsenring and G Wistow (eds) *Developing Quality in Personal Social Services: Concepts, cases and comments.* European Centre, Vienna, pp 63–80.

Bewley C, Glendinning C (1994) *Involving Disabled People in Community Care Planning.* Joseph Rowntree Foundation/*Community Care* magazine, York.

Biggs S, Phillipson C (1992) *Understanding Elder Abuse: A training manual for helping professionals.* Longman, Harlow.

Biggs S, Phillipson C, Kingston P (1995) *Elder Abuse in Perspective.* Open University Press, Buckingham.

Birkett K (1996) *Empowering Older People Seminar,* 15 August, Devizes, Wiltshire and Swindon Users Network, Devizes.

Brand D (1997) General Social Services Council, Service Users Demand Their Say, Press release for Service Users' Conference July 14, National Institute for Social Work, London.

Campbell P (1996) 'The history of the user movement in the United Kingdom', in T Heller, J Reynolds, R Gomm, R Muston and S Pattison (eds) *Mental Health Matters*. Macmillan, Basingstoke.

Croft S, Beresford P (1990) 'Listening to the voice of the service user: a new model for social services research', *Convergence: the Journal of the International Council for Adult Education*, 23(4): 62–68.

Croft S, Beresford P (1992) 'The politics of participation', *Critical Social Policy*, Autumn (35): 20–44.

George J (1994) 'Racial aspects of elder abuse', in M Eastman (ed) *Old Age Abuse: A new perspective*, 2nd edition. Age Concern England/ Chapman & Hall, London.

Harding T (1997) *A Life Worth Living: The independence and inclusion of older people*. Help the Aged, London.

Harding T, Beresford P (eds) (1996) *The Standards We Expect: What service users and carers want from social services workers*. National Institute for Social Work, London.

Jones C (1996) 'Anti-intellectualism and the peculiarities of British social work education', in N Parton (ed) *Social Theory, Social Change and Social Work*. Routledge, London.

King S (1997) *Childhood Matters: The report of the National Commission of Inquiry into the Prevention of Child Abuse, Summary, Childhood Matters Implementation Initiative*. National Society for the Prevention of Cruelty to Children, London.

Lewisham Older Women's Network and the SAVE Project (1995) *Informing Ourselves ... so that we can Empower Others*, report of an Information Day on Elder Abuse, Support and Advice for Vulnerable Adults Project. Lewisham Social Services, London.

McCreadie C (1996a) *Elder Abuse: Update on research*. Age Concern Institute of Gerontology, London.

McCreadie C (ed) (1996b) *Elder Abuse: New perspectives and ways forward*, report of two ageing update conferences. Age Concern Institute of Gerontology, London.

Morris J (1993) *Independent Lives: Community care and disabled people*. Macmillan, Basingstoke.

Oliver M (1996) *Understanding Disability: From theory to practice*. Macmillan, Basingstoke.

Oliver M, Zarb G (1992) *Personal Assistance Schemes in Greenwich: An evaluation*. Greenwich Association of Disabled People, London.

Pfeiffer N, Coote A (1991) *Is Quality Good For You? A critical review of quality assurance in welfare services*, Social Policy Paper No 5. Institute for Public Policy Research, London.

Phillipson C (1994) 'Elder abuse and neglect: social and policy issues', in P Kingston (ed) *Action on Elder Abuse, Working Paper No 1: A report on the proceedings of the 1st International Symposium on Elder Abuse*. Action on Elder Abuse, London, pp 21–27.

Pritchard J (1992) *The Abuse of Elderly People: A handbook for professionals*. Jessica Kingsley, London.

Riseborough M (1996) *Listening To and Involving Older Tenants*. Anchor Trust, Kidlington.

SAVE Project (1996) *Working with Abused Elders and their Families in Lewisham*. Second year event: *Support and Advice for Vulnerable Adults Project*. Lewisham Social Services, London.

Schlesinger B, Schlesinger R (eds) (1988) *Abuse of the Elderly: Issues and annotated bibliography*. University of Toronto Press, Toronto.

Shaping Our Lives Project (1997) *Shaping Our Lives*, video. Healthcare Productions for National Institute for Social Work, London.

Slater P (1992) 'Elder abuse and professional power', *Action on Elder Abuse Bulletin*, 10 (March/April): 2–3.

Social Services Inspectorate (1992) *Confronting Elder Abuse*. HMSO, London.

Social Services Inspectorate (1994) *Abuse of Older People in Domestic Settings: A report on two seminars.* Department of Health, London.

Stevenson O (1996a) *Elder Protection in the Community: What can we learn from child protection?* Age Concern Institute of Gerontology, London.

Stevenson O (1996b) *Elder Protection: What we can learn from child protection in the community?* Summary of report published by the Age Concern Institute of Gerontology, London, and distributed to conference delegates, in *New Perspectives and Ways Forward* – report of two ageing update conferences. Age Concern Institute of Gerontology, London.

Thornton P, Tozer R (1994) *Involving Older People in Planning and Evaluating Community Care: A review of initiatives.* Social Policy Research Unit, University of York, York.

Thornton P, Tozer R (1995) *Having a Say in Change: Older people and community care.* Joseph Rowntree/*Community Care* magazine, York.

Tozer R (1995) *Older People Having a Say in Community Care.* Social Policy Research Unit, University of York, York.

Tozer R, Thornton P (1995) *A Meeting of Minds: Older people as research advisers*, Report No 3. Social Policy Research Unit, University of York, York.

Turner M (1997a) 'Shaping up', *Community Care*, 29 May–4 June, Supplement: 8.

Turner M (1997b) *Interim Report to the Department of Health, Shaping Our Lives Project.* National Institute for Social Work, London.

Wolf RS (1994) 'Responding to elder abuse in the USA', in P Kingston (ed) *Action on Elder Abuse, Working Paper No 1: A report on the proceedings of the 1st International Symposium on Elder Abuse.* Action on Elder Abuse, London, pp 11–19.

Wolf RS, Pillemer KA (1989) *Helping Elderly Victims: The reality of elder abuse.* Columbia University Press, New York.

6 ELDER ABUSE AND PROFESSIONAL INTERVENTION: A SOCIAL WELFARE MODEL?

Aitken L, Griffin G (1996) *Gender Issues in Elder Abuse*. Sage, London.

Association of Directors of Social Services (1995) *Mistreatment of Older People: A discussion document*. ADSS, London.

Baker A (1975) 'Granny battering', *Modern Geriatrics*, 5(8): 20–24.

Bennett G, Kingston P (1993) *Elder Abuse: Concepts, theories and interventions*. Chapman & Hall, London.

Black T (1993) *Evaluating Social Science Research*. Sage, London.

Burston G (1975) 'Granny-battering', *British Medical Journal*, 3: 592.

Department of Health (1992) *Confronting Elder Abuse*. HMSO, London.

Department of Health (1995) *Child Protection: Messages from research*. HMSO, London.

Eastman M (1984) *Old Age Abuse*. Age Concern England, London.

Eastman M (1994) *Old Age Abuse: A new perspective*, 2nd edition. Age Concern England/Chapman & Hall, London.

Holman B (1993) *A New Deal for Social Welfare*. Lion Publishing, Oxford.

Lord Chancellor's Department (1997) *Who Decides? Making decisions on behalf of mentally incapacitated adults*. Stationery Office, London.

McCreadie C (1996a) *Elder Abuse: Update on research*. Age Concern Institute of Gerontology, London.

McCreadie C (ed) (1996b) *Elder Abuse: New perspectives and ways forward*. Age Concern Institute of Gerontology, London.

Parton N (1985) *The Politics of Child Abuse*. Macmillan, London.

Parton N (1995) 'Future Prospects for Child Welfare and Child Protection', Paper delivered to the National Child Protection Co-ordinators' Symposium, Leicester, 24–25 May.

Phillipson C (1982) *Capitalism and the Construction of Old Age*. Macmillan, London.

Raynor P (1985) *Social Work, Justice and Control*. Blackwell, Oxford.

Stanley L, Wise S (1993) *Breaking Out Again*. Routledge, London.

Stevenson O (1996a) *Elder Protection in the Community: What can we learn from child protection?* Age Concern Institute of Gerontology, London.

Stevenson O (1996b) 'Elder protection: what can we learn from child protection in the community?', in C McCreadie (ed) *Elder Abuse: New perspectives and ways forward*. Age Concern Institute of Gerontology, London.

Tomlin S (1989) *Abuse of Elderly People: An unnecessary and preventable problem*. British Geriatric Society, London.

Valios N (1997) 'Inspection abuse', *Community Care*, 17 July: 11.

7 ELDER ABUSE AND SOCIAL WORK: INTEGRATED LEARNING AT QUALIFYING LEVEL

Action on Elder Abuse (1995) *Everybody's Business: Taking action on elder abuse*. AEA, London.

Association of Directors of Social Services (1991) *Adults at Risk: Guidance for directors of social services*. ADSS, Stockport.

Association of Directors of Social Services (1995) *Mistreatment of Older People: A discussion document*, ADSS, Northallerton.

Association of Metropolitan Authorities (1995) *Community Care Legislation*, Social Services Circular 74/1995. AMA, London.

Baldock J, Ungerson C (1994) *Becoming Consumers of Community Care: Households within the mixed economy of welfare*. Joseph Rowntree Foundation, York.

Biggs S, Phillipson C (1992) *Understanding Elder Abuse: A training manual for helping professionals*. Longman, Harlow.

Biggs S, Phillipson C (1994) 'Elder abuse and neglect: developing training programmes', in M Eastman (ed) *Old Age Abuse: A new perspective*, 2nd edition. Age Concern England/Chapman & Hall, London.

Biggs S, Phillipson C, Kingston P (1995) *Elder Abuse in Perspective.* Open University Press, Buckingham.

CCETSW (1991a) *Improving Standards in Practice Learning: Regulations and guidance for the approval of agencies and the accreditation and training of practice teachers,* Paper 26.3, revised edition. Central Council for Education and Training in Social Work, London.

CCETSW (1991b) *Rules and Requirements for the Diploma in Social Work (DipSW),* Paper 30, 2nd edition. Central Council for Education and Training in Social Work, London.

CCETSW (1992) *The Requirements for Post Qualifying Education and Training in the Personal Social Services: A framework for continuing professional development,* Paper 31, revised edition. Central Council for Education and Training in Social Work, London.

CCETSW (1995) *Assuring Quality in the Diploma in Social Work. 1: Rules and Requirements for the DipSW,* revised edition. Central Council for Education and Training in Social Work, London.

CCETSW (1996a) *Assuring Quality for Agencies Approved for Practice Learning: Approval, review and inspection of agencies approved to provide practice learning opportunities for DipSW students.* Central Council for Education and Training in Social Work, London.

CCETSW (1996b) *Assuring Quality for Practice Teaching: Rules and requirements for the practice teaching award/approval, review and inspection of practice teaching programmes.* Central Council for Education and Training in Social Work, London.

Clark H, Dyer S, Horwood J (1998) *That Bit of Help: The high value of low level preventative services for older people.* Policy Press, Bristol.

Coulshed V (1988) 'Curriculum designs for social work education: some problems and possibilities', *British Journal of Social Work,* 18(2): 155–169.

Crow L (1996) 'Including all of our lives: renewing the social model of disability', in C Barnes and G Mercer (eds), *Exploring the Divide: Illness and disability.* Disability Press, Leeds.

Department of Health (1989) *Caring for People: Community care in the next decade and beyond*, Cm 849. HMSO, London.

Department of Health (1991) *Care Management and Assessment: Practitioners' guide*. HMSO, London.

Department of Health (1993) *No Longer Afraid: The safeguard of older people in domestic settings*, Practice Guidelines. HMSO, London.

Department of Health (1995) *Abuse of Older People in Domestic Settings: A report on two SSI seminars*. DoH, London.

Department of Health and Social Security (1986) *Mental Health Act 1983: Approved social workers*, Circular LAC(86)15. HMSO, London.

Eastman M (1984) *Old Age Abuse*. Age Concern England, London.

Goudie F, Alcott D (1994) 'Perspectives in training: assessment and intervention issues in old age abuse', in M Eastman (ed) *Old Age Abuse: A new perspective*, 2nd edition. Age Concern England/Chapman & Hall, London.

Hargreaves S, Hughes B (1996) 'The abuse of older people: an evaluation of the care management model and the impact of anti-discriminatory practice', *Practice*, 8(3): 19–30.

Home Office, Department of Health, Department of Education and Science, Welsh Office (1991) *Working Together under the Children Act 1989: A guide to arrangements for inter-agency co-operation for the protection of children from abuse*. HMSO, London.

Iveson C (1990) *Whose Life? Community care of older people and their families*. Brief Therapy Press, London.

Keller B (1996) 'A model abuse prevention training program for long-term care staff', in L Baumhover and S Beall (eds) *Abuse, Neglect, and Exploitation of Older Persons: Strategies for intervention*. Jessica Kingsley, London.

Kingston P, Penhale B, Bennett G (1995) 'Is elder abuse on the curriculum? The relative contribution of child abuse, domestic violence and elder abuse in social work, nursing and medicine qualifying curricula', *Health and Social Care in the Community*, 3(6): 353–362.

Law Commission (1995) *Mental Incapacity*, Report No 231. HMSO, London.

Levick P (1992) 'The Janus face of community care legislation: an opportunity for radical possibilities', *Critical Social Policy*, 12(1): 75–92.

Lewis J, Glennerster H (1996) *Implementing the New Community Care*. Open University Press, Buckingham.

London Borough of Brent (1985) *A Child in Trust: The report of the panel of inquiry into the circumstances surrounding the death of Jasmine Beckford*. Kingswood, London.

London Borough of Enfield (1990) *Approval of Agencies Providing Practice Learning Opportunities: Stage Two submission to the Central Council for Education and Training in Social Work for full approval*. LBE Social Services Department, London.

London Borough of Enfield (1996) *CCETSW-Approved DipSW Practice Learning Agency Brochure*. Enfield Social Services Group, London.

Ministry of Health (1959) *Report of the Working Party on Social Workers in the Local Authority Health and Welfare Services*. HMSO, London.

Morris J (1993) *Independent Lives? Community Care and Disabled People*. Macmillan, Basingstoke.

O'Leary E (1996) *Counselling Older Adults: Perspectives, approaches and research*. Chapman & Hall, London.

Oliver M (1996) *Understanding Disability: From theory to practice*. Macmillan, Basingstoke.

Penhale B (1993) 'The abuse of elderly people: considerations for practice', *British Journal of Social Work*, 23(2): 95–111.

Pillemer K, Hudson B (1993) 'A model abuse prevention program for nursing assistants', *The Gerontologist*, 33(1): 128–131.

Pritchard J (1995) *The Abuse of Older People: A training manual for detection and prevention*, 2nd edition. Jessica Kingsley, London.

Pritchard J (1996) *Working with Elder Abuse: A training manual for home care, residential and day care staff*. Jessica Kingsley, London.

Scrutton S (1990) 'Ageism: the foundation of age discrimination', in E McEwen (ed) *Age: The unrecognised discrimination*. Age Concern England, London.

Sheppard M (1995) *Care Management and the New Social Work: A critical analysis*. Whiting & Birch, London.

Sinclair I, Parker R, Leat D, Williams J (1990) *The Kaleidoscope of Care: A review of research on welfare provision for elderly people*. HMSO, London.

Slater P (1992) 'What's in it for practice agencies? Joint provision of social work education and training', *Journal of Training and Development*, 2(3): 41–46.

Slater P (1996a) 'Practice teaching and self-assessment: promoting a culture of accountability in social work', *British Journal of Social Work*, 26(2): 195–208.

Slater P (1996b) 'Protection for older people: beyond the elder/adult divide,' *Elders*, 5(3): 12–19.

Smale G, Tuson G with Biehal N, Marsh P (1993) *Empowerment, Assessment, Care Management and the Skilled Worker*. HMSO, London.

Smale G, Tuson G, Ahmad B et al (1994) *Negotiating Care in the Community: The implications of research findings on community based practice for the implementation of the Community Care and Children Acts*. HMSO, London.

Vass T (ed) (1996) *Social Work Competences: Core knowledge, values and skills*. Sage, London.

Winner M (1992) *Quality Work with Older People: Developing models of good practice*. CCETSW, London.

Yelloly M, Henkel M (eds) (1995) *Learning and Teaching in Social Work: Towards reflective practice*. Jessica Kingsley, London.

Zlotnick A (1993) 'Training strategies for elder abuse/inadequate care', *Journal of Elder Abuse & Neglect*, 5(2): 55–62.

Zlotnick A (1995) 'Training on elder abuse', *Action on Elder Abuse Bulletin*, 10: 3–4.

8 ELDER ABUSE IN CARE AND NURSING SETTINGS: DETECTION AND PREVENTION

Alzheimer's Disease Society (1997) *Experiences of Care in Residential and Nursing Homes. A survey.* ADS, London.

Bright L (1997) *Harm's Way.* Counsel and Care, London.

Craft A (1996) 'Abuse of younger and older people: similarities and differences', in R Clough (ed) *The Abuse of Care in Residential Institutions.* Whiting & Birch, London.

Department of Health (1989a) *Homes are for Living In.* HMSO, London.

Department of Health (1989b) *Caring for People: Community care in the next decade and beyond.* HMSO, London.

Department of Health (1994a) *The F Factor.* HMSO, London.

Department of Health (1994b) *Inspecting Social Services*, LAC(94)16. HMSO, London.

Eastman M (1984) *Old Age Abuse.* Age Concern England, Mitcham.

Eastman M (1994) 'The victims: older people and their carers in a domestic setting', in M Eastman (ed) *Old Age Abuse: A new perspective.* Age Concern England/Chapman & Hall, London.

Inman P, Sone K (1997) 'Homes on the range', *Nursing Times*, 93(33): 24–27.

Jenkins D (1997) 'From hell hole to heaven', *Nursing Times*, 93(33): 27–29.

McCreadie C (1996) *Elder Abuse: Update on research.* Age Concern Institute of Gerontology, London.

Nolan M (1996) 'The abuse of care: the relationship between the person and the place', in R Clough (ed) *The Abuse of Care in Residential Institutions.* Whiting & Birch, London.

Parker H (ed) (1996) *Modest – but Adequate – Budgets for Four Pensioner Housholds: October 1994 prices.* Age Concern England/Family Budget Unit Ltd, London.

Public Concern at Work (1997) *Abuse in Care – A necessary reform.* PCW, London.

Valios N (1997) 'Inspection abuse', *Community Care*, 17 July: 11.

9 LEARNING FROM OTHERS: ELDER ABUSE IN INTERNATIONAL PERSPECTIVE

Beaulieu M (1992) 'Elder abuse: levels of scientific knowledge in Quebec', *Journal of Elder Abuse & Neglect*, 4(1/2): 135–149.

Block BE, Sinnott J (eds) (1979) *The Battered Elder Syndrome: An exploratory study.* Center on Aging, University of Maryland, College Park MD.

Cooper AJ, Mendonca JD (1989) 'A prospective study of patient assault on nursing staff in a psychogeriatric unit', *Canadian Journal of Psychiatry*, 34(5): 399–404.

Coyne AC, Reichman WE, Berbig LJ (1993) 'The relationship between dementia and elder abuse', *American Journal of Psychiatry*, 150(4): 643–646.

Eastman M, Slater P, Wahlstrom G (eds) (1997) *Abuse of Older People in Residential Care: A European project.* London Borough of Enfield, London.

Fulmer T, Gurland B (1996) 'Restrictions as elder mistreatment: differences between caregiver and elder perceptions'. *Journal of Mental Health and Aging*, 2(2): 89–100.

Gilleard C (1994) 'Physical abuse in homes and hospitals', in M Eastman (ed) (1994) *Old Age Abuse: A new perspective.* Age Concern England/Chapman & Hall, London, pp 93–110.

Goodridge DM, Johnston P, Thomson M (1996) 'Conflict and aggression as stressors in the work environment of nursing assistants: implications for institutional elder abuse', *Journal of Elder Abuse & Neglect*, 8(1): 49–67.

Grafström M, Norberg A, Winblad B (1993a) 'Abuse is in the eye of the beholder. Reports by family-members about abuse of demented persons in home care. A total population-based study', *Scandinavian Journal of Social Medicine*, 21: 247–255.

Grafström M, Norberg A, Hagberg B (1993b) 'Relationships between demented elderly people and their families: a follow up study of caregivers who had previously reported abuse when caring for their spouses and parents', *Journal of Advanced Nursing*, 18: 1747–1757.

Halicka M (1995) 'Elder abuse and neglect in Poland', *Journal of Elder Abuse & Neglect*, 6: 157–169.

Horkan EM (1995) 'Elder abuse in the Republic of Ireland', *Journal of Elder Abuse & Neglect*, 6: 119–137.

Hydle I (1993) 'Abuse and neglect of the elderly – a Nordic perspective. Report from a Nordic research project', *Scandinavian Journal of Social Medicine*, 21: 126–128.

Hydle I (ed) (1994) *Abuse of the Elderly* (Swedish and Norwegian, with a summary in English), Nord 1994:2. Nordic Councils of Ministers, Köpenhamn.

Hydle I, Johns S (1992) *Closed Doors and Clenched Fists: Elder abuse within the family* (Norwegian). Kommuneforlaget, Oslo.

Jansen B (1995) 'Abuse of the elderly in the Netherlands: policy and experience of combating abuse of the elderly', *Social Work in Europe*, 2: 18–24.

Johns S, Hydle I, Aschjem Ö (1991) 'The act of abuse: a two-headed monster of injury and offence', *Journal of Elder Abuse & Neglect*, 3: 53–64.

Johns S, Hydle I, Juklestad O (1994) 'From not knowing to Elder Protective Service' (Norwegian), in I Hydle (ed) *Abuse of the Elderly* (Swedish and Norwegian), Nord 1994:2. Nordic Councils of Ministers, Köpenhamn, pp 95–105.

Kivelä S-L (1994) 'Elder abuse in Finland', *Journal of Elder Abuse & Neglect*, 6(3/4): 31–44.

Kivelä S-L, Köngäs-Saviaro P, Kesti E et al (1992) 'Abuse in old age – epidemiological data from Finland', *Journal of Elder Abuse & Neglect*, 4: 1–18.

Lau EE, Kosberg JI (1979) 'Abuse of the elderly by informal care providers', *Aging*, 299: 10–15.

Lee-Treweek G (1994) 'Bedroom abuse: the hidden work in a nursing home', *Generations Review*, 4(1): 2–4.

McCreadie C (1996) *Elder Abuse: Update on research*. Age Concern Institute of Gerontology, London.

Meddaugh DI (1993) 'Covert elder abuse in nursing homes', *Journal of Elder Abuse & Neglect*, 5(3): 21–37.

National Board of Health and Welfare (1994) *Abuse of the Elderly in their Homes. Is it the tip of an iceberg?* (Swedish), SoS-report 1994:1. National Board of Health and Welfare, Stockholm.

National Board of Health and Welfare (1995) *Abuse of the Elderly in Residential Settings* (Swedish), SoS-report 1995:4. National Board of Health and Welfare, Stockholm.

National Board of Health and Welfare (1996) *Reporting of Abuse within the Council's Care for the Elderly and Handicapped, including associated health care and nursing care* (Swedish), General Guidance/Circular, SOSFS 1996:11 (S). National Board of Health and Welfare, Stockholm.

Ochotorena JP, Larrión Zugasti JL (1995) 'Elder abuse in Spain', *Social Work in Europe*, 2: 11–14.

Odén B (1991) 'The elderly as a theme in historical research' (Swedish). *Socialmedicinsk Tidskrift*, 68: 64–68.

Odén B (1994) 'Violence against parents in earlier Swedish society' (Swedish), in I Hydle (ed) *Abuse of the Elderly* (Swedish and Norwegian), Nord 1994:2. Nordic Councils of Ministers, Köpenhamn, pp 35–44.

Ogg J (1995) 'Elder abuse in France', *Social Work in Europe*, 2: 8–11.

O'Loughlin A (1995) 'Elder abuse: a perspective from Ireland', *Social Work in Europe*, 2(3): 24–29.

Pillemer K (1988) 'Maltreatment of patients in nursing homes: overview and research agenda', *Journal of Health and Social Behavior*, 29(Sept): 227–238.

Pillemer K, Bachman-Prehn R (1991) 'Helping and hurting. Predictors of maltreatment of patients in nursing homes', *Research on Aging*, 13(1): 74–95.

Pillemer K, Finkelhor D (1988) 'The prevalence of elder abuse: a random sample survey', *The Gerontologist*, 28(1): 51–57.

Pillemer K, Hudson B (1993) 'A model abuse prevention program for nursing assistants', *The Gerontologist*, 33(1): 128–131.

Pillemer K, Moore DW (1989) 'Abuse of patients in nursing homes: findings from a survey of staff', *The Gerontologist*, 29(3): 314–320.

Pillemer K, Moore DW (1990) 'Highlights from a study of abuse of patients in nursing homes', *Journal of Elder Abuse & Neglect*, 2(1/2): 5–29.

Pitsiou-Darrough EN, Spinellis CD (1995) 'Mistreatment of the elderly in Greece', *Journal of Elder Abuse & Neglect*, 6: 45–64.

Podnieks E (1992) 'National survey on abuse of the elderly in Canada', *Journal of Elder Abuse & Neglect*, 4(1-2): 5–58.

Reinharz S (1986) 'Loving and hating one's elders: twin themes in legend and literature', in KA Pillemer and RS Wolf (eds) *Elder Abuse. Conflict in the family*. Dover/Auburn House, Massachussetts, pp 25–48.

Ripamonti E (1995) 'Abuse against the elderly in Italy: a hidden phenomenon', *Social Work in Europe*, 2: 15–17.

Saveman B-I (1994) *Formal Carers in Health Care and the Social Services Witnessing Abuse of the Elderly in their Homes*, Umeå University Medical Dissertations, New series No 403, Umeå University, Umeå.

Saveman B-I, Norberg A (1993) 'Cases of elder abuse, interventions and hopes for the future, as reported by home service personnel', *Scandinavian Journal of Caring Sciences*, 7: 21–28.

Saveman B-I, Hallberg IR (1997) 'Interventions in hypothetical elder abuse situations suggested by Swedish formal carers', *Journal of Elder Abuse & Neglect*, 8: 1–19.

Saveman B-I, Norberg A, Hallberg IR (1992) 'The problems of dealing with abuse and neglect of the elderly: interviews with district nurses', *Qualitative Health Research*, 2(3): 302–317.

Saveman B-I, Hallberg IR, Norberg A (1993a) 'Identifying and defining elder abuse, as seen by witnesses', *Journal of Advanced Nursing*, 18: 1393–1400.

Saveman B-I, Hallberg IR, Norberg A, Eriksson S (1993b) 'Patterns of abuse of the elderly in their own homes as reported by district nurses', *Scandinavian Journal of Primary Health Care*, 11: 111–116.

Saveman B-I, Hallberg IR, Norberg A (1996) 'Narratives by district nurses about elder abuse within families', *Clinical Nursing Research – An International Journal*, 5: 220–236.

Saveman B-I, Åström S, Bucht G, Norberg A (1999) 'Elder abuse in residential settings in Sweden', *Journal of Elder Abuse & Neglect*, in press.

Tornstam L (1989) 'Abuse of the elderly in Denmark and Sweden. Results from a population study', *Journal of Elder Abuse & Neglect*, 1: 35–44.

Wierucka D, Goodridge D (1996) 'Vulnerable in a safe place: institutional elder abuse', *Canadian Journal of Nursing Administration*, 4(3): 82–104.

CONCLUSION

Lord Chancellor's Department (1997) *Who Decides? Making decisions on behalf of mentally incapacitated adults*. HMSO, London.

Marx K (1845/1976) 'Theses on Feuerbach', in K Marx and F Engels, *Collected Works*, volume 5. Lawrence & Wishart, London.

APPENDIX

Department of Health (1998) *Modernising Social Services: Promoting independence, improving protection, raising standards*, Cm 4169. HMSO, London.

Lord Chancellor's Department (1997) *Who Decides? Making decisions on behalf of mentally incapacitated adults*, Cm 3803. HMSO, London.

ABOUT AGE CONCERN

Elder Abuse: Critical issues in policy and practice is one of a wide range of publications produced by Age Concern England, the National Council on Ageing. Age Concern cares about all older people and believes that later life should be fulfilling and enjoyable. For too many this is impossible. As the leading charitable movement in the UK concerned with ageing and older people, Age Concern finds effective ways to change that situation.

Where possible, we enable older people to solve problems themselves, providing as much or as little support as they need. Our network of 1,400 local groups, supported by 250,000 volunteers, provides community-based services such as lunch clubs, day centres and home visiting.

Nationally, we take a lead role in campaigning, parliamentary work, policy analysis, research, specialist information and advice provision, and publishing. Innovative programmes promote healthier lifestyles and provide older people with opportunities to give the experience of a lifetime back to their communities.

Age Concern is dependent on donations, covenants and legacies.

Age Concern England
1268 London Road
London SW16 4ER
Tel: 0181-765 7200
Fax: 0181-765 7211

Age Concern Cymru
4th Floor
1 Cathedral Road
Cardiff CF1 9SD
Tel: 01222 371566
Fax: 01222 399562

Age Concern Scotland
113 Rose Street
Edinburgh EH2 3DT
Tel: 0131-220 3345
Fax: 0131-220 2779

Age Concern Northern Ireland
3 Lower Crescent
Belfast BT7 1NR
Tel: 01232 245729
Fax: 01232 235497

PUBLICATIONS FROM AGE CONCERN BOOKS

PROFESSIONAL, POLICY & RESEARCH

Old Age Abuse: A new perspective
Edited by Mervyn Eastman

The second edition of this ground-breaking book provides an overview of current thinking on the causes of old age abuse, examines the consequences and evaluates the value of possible interventions. Above all, *Old Age Abuse* is designed to encourage care professionals and their managers to recognise that the abuse of older people is an aspect of their work that can no longer be denied or ignored.

Co-published with Chapman & Hall

£14.99 0–41248–420–X

The Abuse of Care in Residential Institutions
Edited by Roger Clough

The Abuse of Care explores the state of knowledge of this abuse, and makes a significant contribution to understanding and action. The authors – a mix of academics, experienced practitioners, consultants and policy-makers – set the scale and nature of the problem of abuse alongside the residential task and explore areas such as:

- uncovering abuse
- management response to institutional response
- organisational underpinnings of abuse
- setting and maintaining standards

The Abuse of Care is essential reading for anyone concerned with this vital question – whether as a student, practitioner, manager or policy maker.

£14.99 1–87117–794–4

The Law and Vulnerable Elderly People
Edited by Sally Greengross

This report raises fundamental questions about the way society views and treats older people. The proposals put forward seek to enhance the self-determination and autonomy of vulnerable older people while ensuring that those who are physically or mentally frail are better protected in the future.

£6.50   0–86242–050–4

Age: The unrecognised discrimination
Edited by Evelyn McEwen

This thought-provoking book seeks to highlight the numerous examples of discriminatory practice against older people in the UK and to challenge the passive popular acceptance of ageism. In a series of discursive essays, leading specialists examine evidence of age discrimination within particular fields and outline action points that will help lead to its elimination.

£10.99   0–86242–094–6

The Community Care Handbook: The reformed system explained
Barbara Meredith

Written by one of the country's leading experts, this hugely successful handbook provides a comprehensive overview of the first two years of implementation of the community care reforms and examines how the system has evolved.

£13.99   0–86242–171–3

Baby Boomers: Ageing in the 21st century
Edited by Maria Evandrou

By the year 2026, the number of people aged 60 and over in the UK will have reached 17.5 million. To date, little attention has been paid to exactly who these millennium elders are, and the opportunities and challenges that are likely to confront them. This book examines the social and economic circumstances of the ageing baby boomer generations and the impact they will have on our society. The key issues explored include:

- employment
- finance
- health
- social service provision
- housing
- social security
- future policy options

Will the baby boomer generations be healthier, wealthier and wiser than their predecessors? What can they expect from the welfare state in the year 2030, in terms of pensions and health and social care?

Baby Boomers: Ageing in the 21st century is essential reading for policy makers, managers, health and social care planners, politicians, researchers and everyone concerned with retirement in the future.

£14.95 0–86242–153–5

If you would like to order any of these titles, please write to the address below, enclosing a cheque or money order for the appropriate amount made payable to Age Concern England. Credit card orders may be made on 0181-765 7200.

Mail Order Unit
Age Concern England
1268 London Road
London SW16 4ER

Information Line

Age Concern produces over 40 comprehensive factsheets designed to answer many of the questions older people – or those advising them – may have, on topics such as:

- finding and paying for residential and nursing home care
- money benefits
- finding help at home
- legal affairs
- making a Will
- help with heating
- raising income from your home
- transfer of assets

Age Concern offers a factsheet subscription service that presents all the factsheets in a folder, together with regular updates throughout the year. The first year's subscription currently costs £50; an annual renewal thereafter is £25. Single copies, up to a maximum of five, are available free on receipt of a stamped addressed envelope.

To order your FREE factsheet list, phone 0800 00 99 66 (a free call) or write to:

Age Concern
FREEPOST (SWB 30375)
Ashburton
Devon TQ13 7ZZ

INDEX